ADMINISTRATION
OF
SOCIAL SECURITY

International Labour Office Geneva

First published 1998

ISBN 92-2-110735-3

Author unit: SEC/PDN
Editor: T. Whitaker
Designer: P. Bissaca, E. Fortarezza
Production: International Training Centre of the ILO, Turin, Italy

PREFACE

This manual is one of a series produced by the Social Security Department of the International Labour Office (ILO), Geneva, in conjunction with the International Training Centre of the ILO, Turin.

The manual examines the main components of social security administration and also draws attention to some of the challenges and difficulties faced by social security institutions.

Other publications in the series:

- Social Security Principles
- Social Security Financing
- Pension Schemes
- Social Health Insurance
- A Trainer's Guide

The manuals have been produced primarily for use in countries where social security systems are not yet operational, are undergoing change or need to be improved. In particular, the manuals will be useful in developing countries, countries in transition, and countries undergoing structural change, as they begin the process of setting up new systems of social protection or of improving existing systems.

It should be noted, however, that the information contained in the manuals refers almost entirely to the formal sector and not to the wide range of systems which apply to groups outside the traditional social security system.

It will be appreciated that, in a manual of this size, it is possible to provide only a broad overview of the topic. For the reader needing more extensive or detailed information about social security administration, there may well be a need for additional reading. There is a wide range of publications which deal with administration and management in general and some which deal with social security administration in particular. Some of these are referred to in the additional reading list at the end of the manual.

Thanks are due to all those people — too numerous to mention individually — who have helped in the preparation of this manual.

Should any reader wish to offer comment or feedback on the contents of this or any other manual in the series, please write to:

The International Labour Office,
SEC SOC, 9th Floor,
4 route des Morillons,
CH-1211 GENEVE 22, Switzerland.
Fax (+41.22) 799.7962

TABLE OF CONTENTS

ADMINISTRATION OF SOCIAL SECURITY

MODULE 1:
INTRODUCTORY MODULE

International Labour Office Geneva

MODULE CONTENTS

MODULE 1

INTRODUCTORY MODULE

UNIT 1: How is social security administered?

A. General overview

What should be expected of a social security administration?

Any administration exists for one purpose only — to provide an effective and efficient service to its clients.

In a social security context, "clients" will include the various participants in the scheme — usually those working for an employer — and the employers themselves. Depending on the design of the social security programme, "clients" may also include other sectors of the population such as the self-employed and the non-employed.

There will be rules and regulations to be observed and the administration should apply them impartially and, as will be seen in a later section, there should be clear rights of appeal for those clients and beneficiaries who feel aggrieved by decisions.

Thus the *ideal administration* is one which is both effective *and* efficient, which works alongside its clients, providing help, advice and a first-rate service. But in practice, there are few social security institutions which can claim that there is no room for improvement in the running of their administration.

It must also be remembered that the majority of social security administrations are each responsible for many millions of scheme members. It follows, therefore, that any failures by the administration will potentially have an impact on an enormous number of people.

Neither should it be forgotten that social security schemes deal with individuals, each of whom is entitled to expect the highest standard of service and treatment from the social security institution.

Before going further in this examination of social security administration, it may be useful to provide a reminder of what social security is and what it seeks to achieve.

A widely accepted definition of social security is:

"The protection furnished by society to its members, by a series of public measures, against the economic and social distress that would otherwise be caused by the stoppage or substantial reduction of earnings resulting from: sickness, maternity, employment injury, unemployment, invalidity, old age and death; to provide medical care and to subsidize families with children".

Consistent with this definition, the *aim* of social security could be said to be:

"to ensure that persons who — either temporarily or permanently — are unable to obtain an income, or who are facing exceptional financial responsibilities, are enabled to continue to meet their needs by providing them with financial resources or certain goods or services ..."

It also follows from these that individuals who find themselves in such a situation will require not only efficient and effective help — but *prompt* help. The challenge for all social security administrations is therefore to provide *an efficient, effective and timely service* to all its clients.

It is important that this challenge is born in mind throughout this manual, for it has an impact on all aspects of administration.

Fig. 1:
"... the challenge ...
to provide prompt ...
efficient ...
service to its clients ..."

B. Social security policy

The more widespread the coverage of social security, the greater will be the need for direction of policy by central government. This is to be expected, given that government has the ultimate responsibility for the overall social and economic well-being of the population.

The autonomy of social security institutions is usually confined to administrative matters and decisions concerning issues relating to

- policy

- the contents of legislation

- coverage

- the nature of the benefits to be provided

- the amount of and allocation of funds, within the framework of national economic plans,

will normally be the responsibility of the government and will be set in legislation.

The arrangement which is most commonly found is that a central government department has the overall responsibility for social security. This may be the Ministry of Labour, or Social Services or Health — indeed there may well be a special Ministry for social security itself.

Some countries have a Social Security Commission — or a similarly named body — which is charged with policy making and has the supreme oversight of social security operations but which is still, in the final analysis, responsible to central government.

In other countries, the legislation creates a parastatal body — with a title such as "Social Security Institute", "National Social Security Fund", "National Insurance Board", etc., — which has the responsibility to implement the terms of the laws determined by the responsible Minister.

The degree of independent action open to such a body varies. Some may have the power to engage their own staff and build their own premises, others may rely on secondments from the government; some may have a free hand to invest funds, whilst others may be subject to direction by the finance ministry.

Sometimes, policy making is divided between a number of central government departments. Where such arrangements apply, it is clearly vital that there is close and effective coordination between them.

C. *Structures*

There is no particular or special model, or standard pattern, for social security administrative structures or organization. Given the enormous variation in social security schemes around the world, this is hardly surprising.

Different structures suit different situations and most of today's social security institutions have developed largely on the basis of "what seemed appropriate, at the time, to meet particular needs". They have also adapted over time as schemes have changed and developed.

Most of the structures which are in use at present grew up with a minimum of positive planning, for a combination of reasons — historical, political and social. The earliest schemes — employment injury schemes — were administered by employers, commercial insurance companies and courts of law. Indeed, this pattern continues successfully in some countries today.

Other early structures followed a pattern under which the social insurance legislation provided for sickness and pensions institutes to be managed by representatives of the contributors themselves. This principle was written into some of the early ILO Conventions and there are still countries which depend on this very localized structure.

There are also countries where the gradual achievement of near-universal coverage of the population has been accompanied by the gradual creation of a comprehensive, single institution to manage the social security programme. Yet other countries, perhaps profiting by example, have established their social security programmes under a single national management from the start. In these countries it is usual to find a much more formal structure with the single institution responsible for all aspects of the social security programme, from collection of contributions to the determination and payment of a variety of benefits.

A statutory board is often found at the head of a contributory social insurance scheme or provident fund. The accumulated moneys are vested in the board which acts, in effect, as trustee for the contributors — publishing annual reports and accounts.

A board which is itself responsible for investing funds is also likely to have an investment committee, formed from those of its members who are experienced in this area of financial management. Such a committee would generally include both workers' and employers' representatives and experts from, for example, the finance ministry, development bank or investment consultants.

Because social insurance and provident funds work to closely defined legal rules, it is generally inappropriate for boards to intervene in technical or procedural matters, such matters usually being regarded as the responsibility of the chief executive and his staff. However, with *social assistance*, where officials have more discretion in determining the needs and resources of clients, the board may have to give direction on policy aspects of the day-to-day administration.

In either case, the board will have an influential voice with its parent Ministry in the development of major policy matters.

The Social Security Convention, No.102 (1952) lays down that the member government shall accept general responsibility for the proper administration of the institutions and services concerned with social security. It also requires that, where the administration is delegated away from the government level, the representatives of the protected persons — the scheme's members — should participate in the management or be associated with it in a representative capacity.

Fig. 2:
"Social Security Conventions and Recommendations"

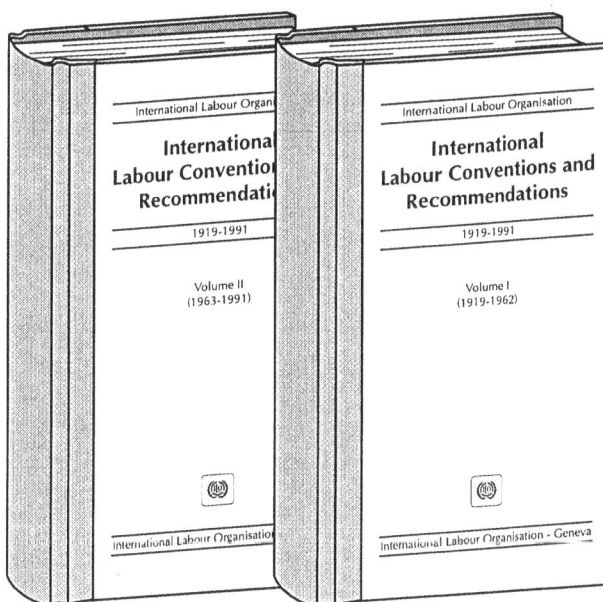

A typical statutory board would fulfil this requirement, for it would be comprised of representatives of employed persons and employers with the addition of officials from the major government departments concerned.

The worker and employer members are usually elected or nominated by the trade unions and employer organizations, respectively, or appointed by the Minister after consultation with those bodies.

Often the director, or permanent head of the social security organization being supervised by the board, will also have a seat on the board itself.

Although, as already pointed out, there is no single, common structure, Figure 3 provides an illustration of what might be regarded as a fairly typical, broad structural overview.

Fig. 3:
"...fairly typical, broad structural overview..."

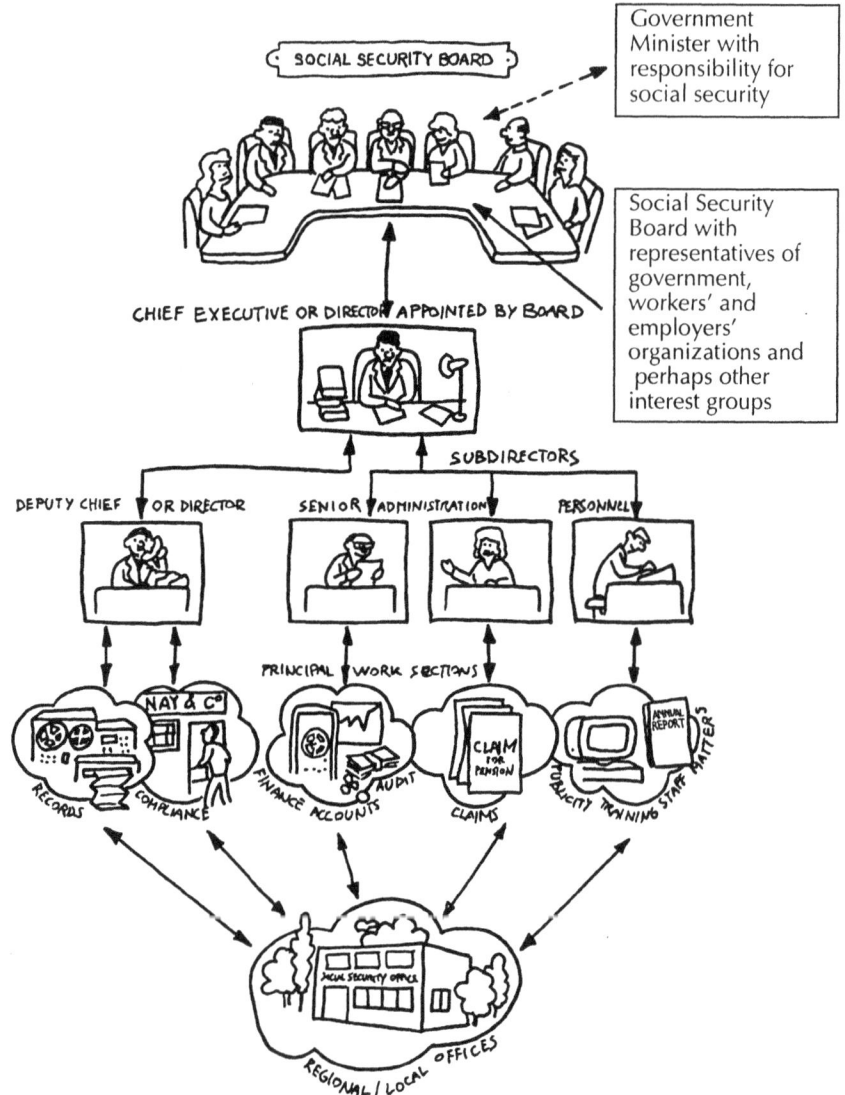

In the situation where the social security administration is *not* delegated but remains in a separate division of the responsible government department, representatives of the scheme members and of employers may be appointed to an advisory committee — not unlike the statutory board but with the simpler function of giving advice to the Minister.

Such a committee would generally advise on matters of policy or administration which might be referred to it by the Minister or which may be raised on the initiative of the committee.

Another way for the scheme members to be associated with the administration of social security is for the responsibility to be devolved, in some degree, from the public authorities to the trade unions.

D. Common features

Regardless of the structural form which the social security administration has developed, all social insurance programmes and provident funds have one thing in common — the need to collect contributions and bring them to account in the personal records of the scheme's members.

The maintenance of accurate, reliable and easily accessible records for such schemes is vitally important, in order to determine benefits due to contributors. Qualifying periods for long-term benefits may extend over many years and properly maintained, detailed, individual records are therefore required.

These requirements have generally resulted in a tendency to maintain records centrally, in order to help in the identification and recording processes, particularly when workers move from one employer or area to another.

Over recent years, however, the rapid development of information technology and of interlinked and networked computer systems has increasingly meant that the centralization of records is no longer of paramount importance. This has been complemented by the development of new systems, relying on modern technology, for the payment of contributions.

As will be explained in more detail later, under the payroll system employers remit contributions directly to the social security institution with details of individual workers (usually at monthly intervals) which are then transferred to the individual members' records.

Regardless of the system being used, an essential requirement is that each worker, employer or other participant must have a unique reference number which is used for as long as he or she has an association with the social security programme. Registration and maintenance of records will be explored more fully in later sections.

Means tested and universal social security schemes do not have the same need to maintain records of employment, or of individual members, contributions, because the qualifying conditions for benefits are normally based on the period of residence rather than on contributions paid and/or length of period(s) of employment. However, the need for efficient maintenance of records is still relevant if only in relation to benefit awards, payments or refusals.

One important feature, common to all social security institutions, is the need for the administration to have the capacity to process, calculate and pay benefits in an accurate and timely manner.

Other common features include: planning functions; financial accounting; financial management; satisfactory compliance with the law, particularly in regard to payment of contributions. These and other aspects will be revisited in subsequent sections as specific administrative activities.

UNIT 2: Levels of administration

A. The local level

As has been seen already, the principal task of any social security organization is to provide prompt, accurate and efficient payment of benefits to members of the scheme. Everything else which the organization does, although necessary, is subordinate to that task.

Social security has to respond to many varieties and combinations of personal circumstances and is therefore a complex operation. It is also "big business", for most schemes handle hundreds of thousands of claims, make millions of benefit payments and deal with huge sums of money in the course of a year.

The organization therefore needs to be able to cope with large numbers and matching demands but at the same time it must be flexible, able to implement changes quickly, and yet deal with each customer on a personal but impartial basis.

The customer — the scheme member — will wish to have easy access to the organization and, ideally, it is the local level at which a member should be able to obtain a personal service, even if the benefit claim has to be sent elsewhere in the organization for processing.

In schemes which have a national network, the local offices vary markedly in number and size. Generally, the aim is to locate them in the main centres of population and for them to be sufficient in number to bring social security facilities within reasonable reach of most of the covered population. This often means that there will be several local offices in heavily populated urban areas, whilst in sparsely populated rural areas they may be few and far between.

Although a local office network may be the *ideal* situation, in many countries it is not a reality because responsibility for administration of the social security scheme has not yet been decentralized. At the early developmental stages of a new scheme, some organizations undertake all the administrative functions from a central office. As the scheme and the organization develops, the next stage in the process of bringing the administration closer to the participants may be to provide an office in each of the country's main regions, provinces, zones or districts. (For ease of reference, these will be referred to, throughout this manual, as "regional offices".) Only if and when further development becomes possible, below that level, would the introduction of a local office network be appropriate.

Where a scheme does succeed in introducing a local level of administration, such offices generally receive benefit claims, give decisions thereon and make consequential payments. Such schemes usually also rely heavily on the local office network for registration of members and employers, for procedures relating to the collection of contributions and for ensuring a satisfactory level of compliance with, and enforcement of, the law — particularly relating to contribution issues.

As will be seen in greater detail in a later section dealing with contribution collection, most schemes depend on social security inspectors to ensure a satisfactory standard of compliance. It is important that they have access to employers and this is helped if inspectors can be based locally — ideally in local offices — so that they become familiar with the locality and with the employers in that locality.

Where a local office network does exist, the offices tend to vary in size and organization. These are influenced by a number of factors including: the size and type of geographical area covered; workload volumes; predominant activities; numbers of staff required, etc. However, the broad organizational structure will be quite similar from one local office to the next, as each will inevitably reflect — though on its own appropriate scale — the work contents and responsibilities of the central or headquarters office, viz. Administration of benefits, contribution collection, finance and administration, personnel, training, etc.

Fig. 4:
*"Where local offices
do exist ...
they inevitably vary in size
and organization ..."*

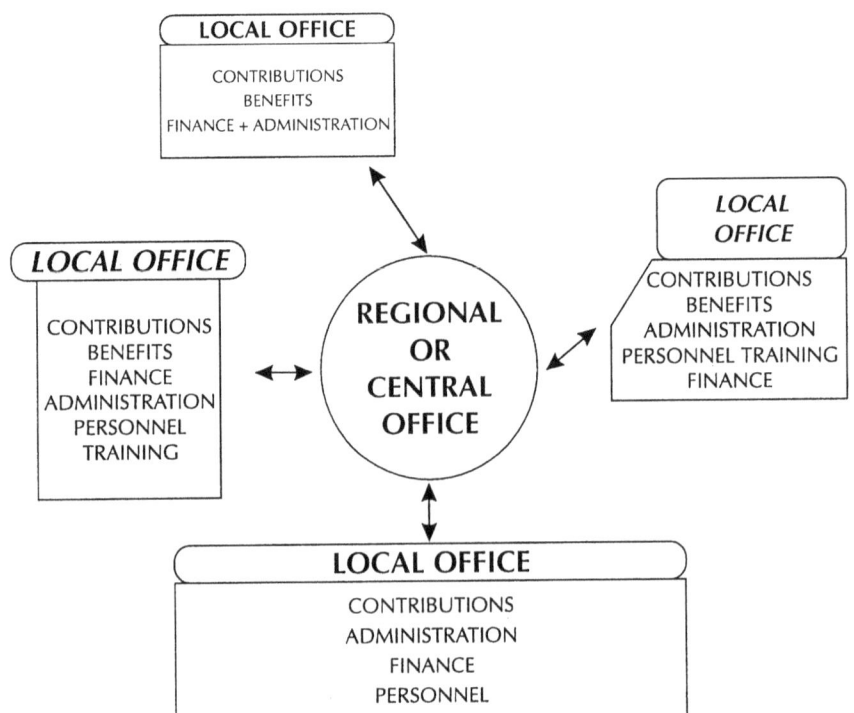

A key feature common to all social security offices (whether at local, district, regional or central level) is the need for a public office, with private interview facilities, which individual members can visit to obtain information and advice, receive assistance with benefit claims, produce documentary evidence in support of those claims, register for membership, etc. A social security office at which members are able to obtain such services usually also needs to be equipped for the payment of cash benefits.

Cash benefits are paid in a variety of ways. They may be paid directly to the member at the social security office or, where the infrastructure supports such systems, they may be paid via banks, post offices, by mail or through direct bank transfers.

Some schemes enlist the help of employers to make payments of certain short-term benefits, followed by reimbursement from the social security organization. Facilities also exist in some schemes to pay to an agent, authorized by the member.

The payment of long-term benefits and pensions often tends to be a centralized operation, with the local/district/regional office playing a part in processing claims whilst having little involvement in the payment mechanism. As with short-term benefits, the method of payment will largely be dictated by the level of development of infrastructure and the financial systems available. These vary considerably with, at one end of the spectrum, highly automated direct transfers through the banking system — perhaps even with the beneficiary using a "smart-card" to obtain cash — and at the other end of the spectrum, monthly payments in cash, by local office staff or their agents, at the local office, or in a local community meeting place, or even at the local market place.

Social security organizations which do have a local office network generally have their own guidelines for determining the number and location of local offices. Clearly a balance has to be found between too many, resulting in large and perhaps unnecessary administrative expenditure, and too few, resulting in an inadequate level of service for those members far removed from their nearest office. This is a difficult balance to achieve.

For small, isolated communities which do not warrant a local office, there is often a need for ingenuity in providing a satisfactory level of service. This issue will be revisited in the section dealing with public relations. Suffice it to say at this point, however, that there is ample scope for imaginative solutions to the problems of providing some form of service to such communities.

Some social security schemes, which operate alongside a health insurance scheme, may have health centres attached to local/district offices — or vice versa. Such a local office may have to receive, check and process accounts for medical services, prescriptions and hospital care, or claims for reimbursement where members have already met the costs. In some cases a dispensary or clinic may be associated with the local office, perhaps even sharing premises and coming under a common management.

From this brief reference to organization at the local level, it will be appreciated that, even where a social security institution *does* have a local office network, there is a wide variety of organizational patterns and range of responsibilities.

B. The "regional" level

In many countries, especially where there are well-defined provincial, regional, district, or zone boundaries, the social security institution's organization will include a "regional" tier, often with an office in each of the main regions. If there is no local office tier, it will usually be the regional offices which are responsible for day-to-day administration of all activities related to collection of contributions and processing of benefit claims.

Where the institution does have a local office network, the major responsibility of a regional office is the general oversight, monitoring and control of the local offices within that region. Regional offices of this type would not normally deal directly with the public although they would almost certainly be involved in some aspects of case-work, for example giving advice to their local offices on the more unusual or complex claims.

All regional offices would be answerable to the central or headquarters office and each would be organized on broadly similar lines, having specialist sections, divisions or departments, each of those being responsible for and dealing with questions on one of the main operational areas — contributions, compliance, benefits, financing, administration, etc. In some of the larger social security institutions, the headquarters office may delegate responsibility to regional offices for staffing (complements, recruitment, reporting, promotions, terminations, etc.) within the region.

The larger the social security organization, the more likely it is that a greater degree of specialization would be found at regional and local levels. Offices at the regional tier which have a large number of staff, an extensive network of local offices to service and a large budget, would probably also need specialist sections dealing with transport, premises and equipment, staff training, new technology, public relations, to name but a few.

Fig. 5:
"... two tier organization ..."

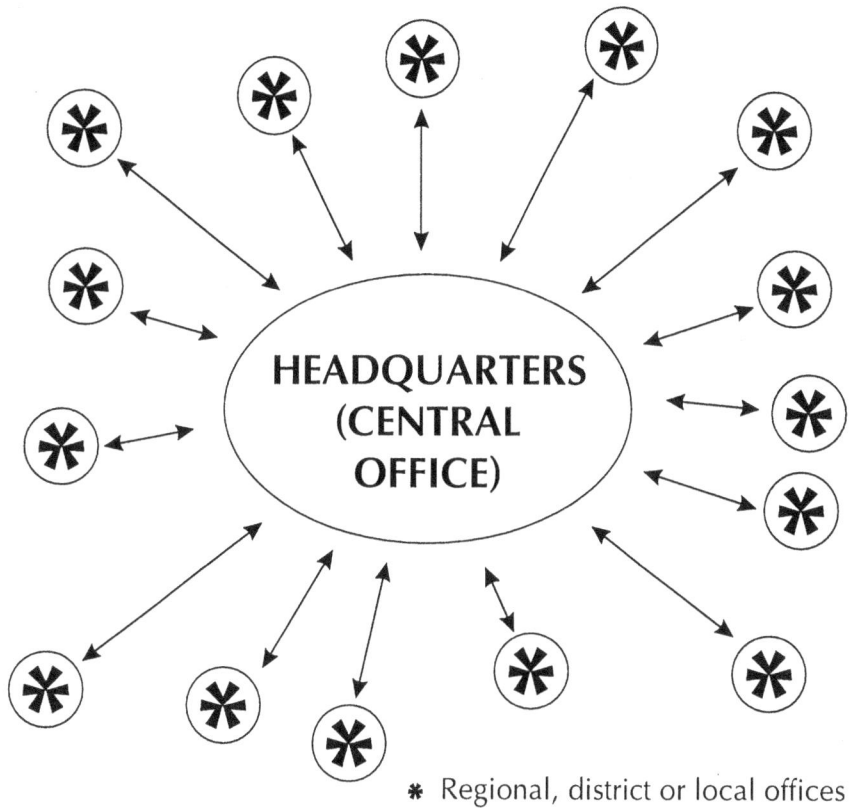

* Regional, district or local offices

Fig. 6:
"... the larger social security institutions may have a three tier organization ... headquarters, regional and local offices ..."

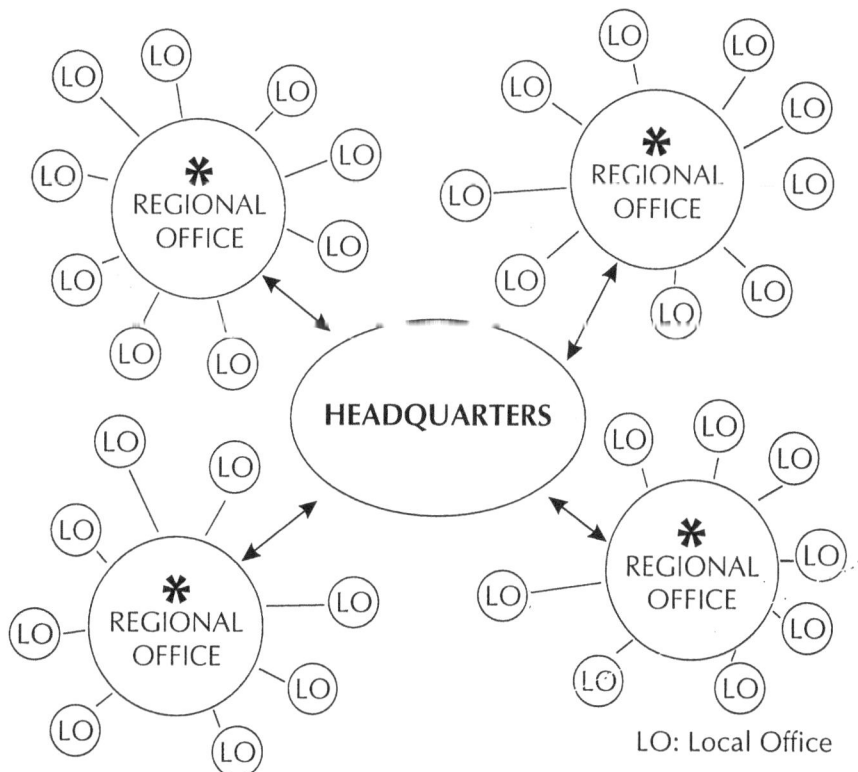

LO: Local Office

C. Headquarters level

Whatever the size of the social security institution, it will usually be headed by a Chief Executive Officer, Managing Director, Director General — or similar title — who will be supported by a group of senior personnel including (as a minimum):

- a Director of Finance, with the ultimate responsibility for all matters relating to finance (budgets, accounts, internal audit, etc.);

- a Contributions Division Director, responsible for all contributions issues (registration, collection, compliance, maintenance of records, etc.); and

- a Benefits Division Director, responsible for all benefits aspects (benefits procedures, adjudication, appeals, etc).

Additionally, in a large-scale organization, the headquarters would be likely to need:

- a Medical Officer, to advise on medical matters and to organize the medical examination of those members claiming invalidity benefit or employment injury benefits;

- a Legal Officer, to handle the questions of interpretation of the law, prosecutions (for fraud, non-compliance, etc.) and the appeal bodies.

Headquarters offices would almost certainly have additional specialist divisions, responsible for the various "housekeeping activities" of the social security organization — staffing, premises, furniture and equipment, stationery, security, public relations.

Other important responsibilities of a headquarters office include:

- research activities;

- advice to ministers, particularly on policy formulation and development;

- interpretation of legislation;

- technical/procedural advice to regional/local offices;

- collection, collation and analysis of statistical* returns from regional/local offices (e.g. intake of benefit claims, new member registrations, work-flow, work processed/outstanding).

---

*The importance of statistics in the management of social security has been emphasized by the ILO in the detailed guidance given in the publication entitled *"Scheme of statistical tables for the practical application of a minimum programme of social security statistics".*

All schemes, regardless of their size and complexity, will need to have an organization which is able to address all the aspects referred to in the preceding paragraphs. The main difference will be one of scale. Large, complex schemes will need all the specializations referred to — and perhaps even more. Medium and small schemes will need only some or may perhaps combine several of the functions.

D. New technology

Electronic Data Processing (EDP) systems are increasingly commonplace in social security organizations. The developments in new technology have been — and are likely to continue to be — so rapid that what is new today is dated tomorrow. Computerization programmes have had a major impact on social security operations, not least as a means of collecting, processing and storing information quickly and economically. The computer can also be seen as a way of abolishing routine, monotonous, jobs and as a way of providing rapid access to and retrieval of information which, in turn, gives the public a more reliable and speedy service.

However, there are those who regard the introduction or extension of EDP systems with some anxiety or apprehension. They fear, for example, that some of the information recorded may be incorrect, that members may have no access to records in order to contest inaccuracies. Increasingly, however, legislation is being introduced which gives individuals the right to know what data is being stored about them on their records, and giving them the opportunity to have it changed, corrected and updated. Many countries also have laws which prevent the information being divulged to third parties.

The development of computerized social security systems can also lead to fears amongst the personnel of the social security organization, in particular the fear of redundancies. In developing countries, national policies relating to levels of employment/unemployment sometimes dictate that labour-intensive methods should take precedence over computerized systems.

Developing countries may also have additional problems, such as the need to use hard-earned foreign currency to rent, or buy and install, expensive equipment. A shortage of trained staff may be a problem too, not to mention the retention of such staff as they become increasingly experienced and when — as is often the case — they find they can command higher rates of pay in the private sector.

It is sometimes tempting for social security organizations, which are unable to afford to install computer systems of their own, to buy time with private, commercial computer companies. There are a number of dangers in such arrangements and a number of factors to consider, including the following: what priority will be afforded to the social security service; what protection will there be for the data, particularly confidential or sensitive personal data about members; how easy will it be for the social security organization to retrieve information and data, either when processing benefit claims or when eventually installing its own computerized system?

It is wise, when considering the introduction of computerized social security systems, to take advice from those who are experienced in the computerization of social security — rather than from those who are *only* experienced in computerization but have no knowledge of social security systems and procedures.

Social security institutions which are still using manual procedures should recognize and accept the inevitability of computerization at some future point in time. With this in mind it is essential that, in the meantime, the introduction, development, and modification of manual procedures must be designed to facilitate the eventual change to an EDP (computerized) system.

It is also vital, once the process of computerization begins, that there is a very close working relationship and ongoing dialogue between the staff of the EDP division and "the users" — the staff and managers in the departments whose procedures are to be computerized. As computerized systems are developed to replace manual operations, it is essential that users have opportunities for input, for they are the people who best understand the manual processes and their related problems. If computer experts fail to obtain user input, there is a risk that new problems will simply replace old ones.

Earlier reference was made to the speed of change in the computerization field. Bearing that fact in mind, it is important to ensure that the most up-to-date features of computerized social security systems are built into new installations. It may therefore be useful for the EDP division's senior personnel to obtain information and advice from institutions which already have long established and well developed EDP systems. This is one of the aspects of social security development which the ILO has been heavily involved in, over a number of years, through its technical cooperation projects.

One of the central aims of a new social security EDP development should be the provision of an "on-line system" for the transmission and retrieval of data. This enables staff, at any of the institution's offices, to transmit information to or retrieve it from the computer data base. The advantages of a comprehensive, fully networked, on-line system are far-reaching. They include, for example, the reduced incidence of duplicate or multiple registrations, speedier allocation of paid contributions, quicker identification of non-compliance and much shorter processing times for benefit claims.

These are clearly major advantages for the institution but, in order to safeguard them, it is vital that the computerized data base is frequently updated. Programmes must always, therefore, be designed to accommodate regular inputs of up-to-date information to data base records.

Whether embarking on an EDP programme for the first time, or extending existing systems, institutions should remember that prices in the computer hardware and software markets are becoming increasingly competitive. Nevertheless, given the volume of equipment required by even the smallest social security institution, the expenditure will still be substantial. It is important, therefore, that prices are closely checked and that competitive bidding procedures are used, wherever possible.

Reference is made elsewhere in this manual to the possibility of developing computer links with employers in order to facilitate the transfer of contribution remittances and schedules. It can be mutually advantageous if this type of link can be extended to other organizations, for example, banks, post offices, and any others with whom a working relationship exists. Computer links may also be of use with other government departments, for example the tax authorities.

Finally, it must be remembered that the introduction of computers does not in itself overcome basic problems of poorly designed programmes and systems. Indeed, sometimes manual back-up procedures may be needed, running alongside the computerized system, as a safety feature in the event of systems failures.

UNIT 3: Principles of good management in social security institutions

A. The importance of good management practices

It will have been apparent, from previous units, that social security institutions vary markedly in size, range of tasks and responsibilities, complexity, and the way they are organized. It will be equally clear, however, that the demands placed on managers of social security institutions will in many ways be very similar, regardless of the size of the organization. They all share similar objectives, not least the key objective of providing their clients with an efficient and effective service. Another common requirement for all social security administrations is the need to design, adopt and maintain good management practices. This cannot be over-emphasized.

Reference has already been made to the need for an administration which is effective and efficient. Such administrations don't "just happen" — they need to be developed. That development depends on people, and the institution will only be as good as the people who work for it.

Principles of good management are much the same for social security institutions as for most other organizations, whether in the public or private sector. The principles of management are, of course, quite unlike the principles of mathematics or the laws of the natural sciences. Indeed, in the management field, there is no universal agreement as to what the principles are, nor can it be said that the principles are valid for *all* situations. Indeed, there is a case to be made for not using the term "management principles" but to use instead "management guidelines" — which are, simply, potentially useful generalizations about factors which make for success in management.

Nevertheless, it is perhaps useful to be reminded of what the guidelines include, viz. The main elements of "good management" of any organization or institution, including social security institutions.

The following brief reference to some of the most widely recognized guidelines may help to focus attention on key management areas and organizational structure.

- **Span of control**
  Refers to the optimum number of subordinates that an executive can control. As the number of subordinates

increases, so the degree and effectiveness of control decreases.

- **Levels of management**
  Too many levels of management reduce the effectiveness of communication and control.

- **Unity of command**
  Each person should report to only one supervisor/line-manager.

- **Delegation**
  Work must be delegated to subordinates who should then be given sufficient authority to enable them to discharge their responsibilities. It should be remembered, however, that responsibility can be delegated but cannot be relinquished; the executive who delegates a task still remains accountable for its achievement. "Delegation without control is abdication".

- **Rational assignment**
  People should be assigned to tasks rationally and economically, so as to ensure full utilization of manpower.

- **Action decisions**
  Matters requiring a decision should be dealt with as near to the point of action as possible.

- **Line and staff**
  It is desirable to separate the control of operations, as a management function, from the provision of services or advice to the operational units.

Fig. 7:
"... the main elements of good management ..."

It is worth noting that there are a number of commentators, particularly in the field of behavioural science, who have begun to question the universal validity of some of these management guidelines. There is a suggestion that, if adherence to them is *too* strict, there is a risk of increased rigidity of organizations and a consequential reduction in flexibility — particularly where conditions are changing rapidly.

Some additional points, which need to be considered when an organization is designing its overall structure, should also be noted.

Decentralized organizations inevitably have a greater number of managers, as each location requires its own manager and its own management structure. A number of features follow from this. There is a need for more management training — for more people; tight control of local managers is required from the regional or central office; it is essential that there are clear lines of management and a strong management chain. In this form of organization, the "pyramid structure" is typical.

There is an increasing use, in many organizations, of a "mission statement" which is intended to provide a focus for the organization's activities and a platform around which corporate goals and objectives can be built: for example "providing social protection to all eligible citizens in a fair, honest, prompt, efficient and transparent manner — whilst recognizing the rights and equality of all".

Corporate planning requires the organization to produce a corporate plan which establishes the organization's direction for the period ahead, for example the next five to ten years.

B. Effective management of resources

The effective management of resources — both human and physical — is clearly central to all management functions. Organizations are in a constant state of change and development, and it follows that resource management should always be at the forefront of day-to-day management activities.

Manpower planning (a term which is interchangeable with "human resource planning") is a key feature of the management of human resources and involves an analysis of present and projected manpower requirements and the formulation of plans to meet forecast surpluses or (perhaps more commonly in social security institutions) shortfalls.

Human resource management also includes recruitment and selection (to be dealt with in Module 7); pay and conditions; deployment; training (see Module 7); motivation; retention, redundancy and dismissal. Each of these aspects warrants several chapters in their own right but this is clearly not possible in a publication of this nature. Suffice it to say that if any of the aspects is not dealt with effectively, by managers at all levels and in all parts of the organization, then the combined operations of the institution cannot be effective.

The management of physical resources — premises and equipment — is one management function which is easily and often mismanaged; not least because it is such a vast undertaking for most social security institutions. From the construction and ownership, or rental, of buildings to the supply of pens for the staff — and the myriad of resources in between — there are pitfalls which have the potential to put at risk the effectiveness of the management of physical resources. The increasing use of information technology, and the expensive equipment which that requires, makes for a situation where even the smallest miscalculation in resource estimates can be very costly for the organization.

Physical resource management also includes a diverse range of related operational and organizational features, including: office layouts; organization of office services; support services; telephone and fax facilities; copying and reproduction; printing and duplicating; microfilming and fingerprinting procedures in some institutions; security and safety; building maintenance — to name but a few.

Given the range and variety of these elements, the management of physical resources is clearly an aspect which provides an enormous challenge. Most organizations will have a section or department which is specifically responsible for premises, equipment and the overall management of physical resources. It must be remembered, however, that *all* supervisors and managers have a part to play in ensuring that resources *are* managed carefully. Indeed, *everyone* employed by the institution has an individual responsibility to ensure that physical resources are used efficiently and effectively.

C. *Financial controls*

As explained in more detail in the manual on Social Security Financing (Manual No. 3 in this series) most social security schemes provide a combination of short-term, long-term and employment injury benefits, and sometimes operate a provident fund. Different systems of financing apply to each of these benefit branches, and separate accounts of income and expenditure must be maintained for each branch. The funds accumulated in each branch must also be separately recorded. The need for stringent application of rules and procedures in all finance and accounting activities inevitably requires a series of checks and controls.

The controls associated with raising revenue (collecting contributions) are dealt with in Modules 3 and 4. The following paragraphs will therefore focus primarily on the financial controls related to expenditure.

The expenditure of a social security scheme can be broadly divided into benefit payments, investment expenses, and administration expenses. Benefit payments are normally a statutory obligation of the scheme. Investment expenses are generally assessed separately and deducted from gross investment income.

Administration expenses comprise a category of expenditures over which management can exercise effective control and this section of the manual looks mainly at those financial controls for which managers at the operational level are responsible. (A later module will make reference to finance and security aspects of benefit payments.)

Financial planning and control

The first stage in setting up financial systems for an organization is to draw up a financial plan. From this an annual budget can be constructed, against which actual income and expenditure can be monitored.

It is important to have a financial plan which supports the medium or longer term plan for the scheme, covering perhaps a three or five-year period. Although it will be difficult to predict events over this time period, such a plan is essential so as to give some direction to the organization's activities, and also to help clarify its priorities.

Annual budgets have three main purposes:

* Planning:
  in order to quantify the financial effects of the action that is required to achieve the immediate goals and longer term objectives; also determines which of the overall objectives are able to be achieved in the coming financial year.

- Authorisation:
  the approved budget gives the authority to incur expenditure.

- Control:
  the budget becomes the basis of control for income and expenditure and sets the standard against which actual performance can be measured.

Budgetary control   As described, the budget is a quantification of the short-term plan and a forecast of what is expected to be achieved (in financial terms) in the next accounting period.

After the start of the budget period, actual expenditure is incurred and recorded. At the end of each month, accounts are prepared from the records of actual expenditure and it is then possible to compare the budget — the expected expenditure — with the actual expenditure.

It is important that management accountability is established by clarifying which parts of the organization (and the appropriate senior officers) are responsible for income/ expenditure in certain areas, and for the monitoring of that income/expenditure.

For a budgetary control system to operate successfully, it is necessary to report on the planned/actual position throughout the year. The annual budget must be profiled — that is, broken down into monthly (or quarterly) figures. Unless income and expenditure is incurred evenly over the year, dividing the budget by 12 (or four) will not be appropriate. Instead, a budgetary profile should be prepared. This will show the estimate of the proportion of the budget that might be expected to have been used up for each monthly (or quarterly) period.

It is the *profiled* budget which is then compared with the *actual* accounts at the end of each month/quarter. The differences between the budget and the actual expenditure are called *variances* (which can be positive or negative). It is necessary for the organization to determine, during the financial planning process, at what stage the variances become significant; for example it may be at a fixed percentage (e.g. 5%) or at a fixed amount of money. Significant variances can then be investigated to establish their cause, which may be, for example, an inaccurate budget estimate, inaccurate profiling, lack of financial control, unexpected change in activity, etc. When the reason for variance has been determined, appropriate action can be implemented, where necessary.

Budget reports must provide sufficient information for budget holders to be able to act on. However, full and detailed reports for *every* budget item, for *every* division or department, would almost certainly be too cumbersome and could lead to important information being missed, simply because it is hidden amongst the volume of data produced. It is therefore usual to produce a full budget report only periodically, e.g. every quarter, but with *exception reports* being used in between. An exception report shows only the significant variances, thus directing management's attention to the most relevant areas of income/expenditure. This enables the assumption to be made that any item which is not listed on the exception report is in line with the expected pattern.

It is also useful to have a formal budget review process, perhaps at the mid-year point. This enables action to be taken on changing income/expenditure patterns and changing circumstances, and provides an opportunity for budgets to be revised. Once the budget has been profiled, it is relatively simple to produce updated forecasts of income/expenditure for the year. This is done by using the income/expenditure information for the year to date and adding to that the profiled information for the remaining months, making adjustments for any changes that have occurred since the budget was prepared.

The procedure for agreeing these changes should be similar to that for the budget preparation. However, this should *not* be seen as an opportunity to gain agreement for policy changes or new activity; the review is *only* for reflecting changed circumstances.

As a part of this review process — or indeed as an addition to it — *virement* can be applied. A virement is where a saving in one department, or under one cost heading, is transferred to another. Such a transfer usually requires authorization at "an appropriate level", depending on the type or size of the virement. As with all other aspects of financial procedures, it is essential that there are documented regulations for virement, so that it is clear *where* they can be applied, *who* can authorize them and *what* the limits are.

Many public organizations have a *cash limit* applied to their budget. The effect is that, once the budget is approved by the relevant body, the total budget becomes a cash limit which cannot be exceeded (although virement may be permitted). Under cash-limited budgets, if the amount estimated in the budget (for pay awards or inflation, for example) is less than the amount required, the shortfall can *only* be met from other savings or from reserves.

D. Internal auditing

It should be made clear at the outset that this section relates to *financial* auditing and not to other functions which may include "audit" in their title or references; for example, "performance auditing", which is more concerned with the examination and evaluation of organization and methods, and how things are done, rather than with financial or numerical accuracy.

Social security legislation usually requires that annual accounts must be examined and certified by an auditor who is entirely independent of the administering authority. Where a scheme is small, the external audit, supported by internal management checks, may be all that is needed to satisfy the responsible authority that management has discharged its accounting responsibilities.

However, the technical complexities and sheer volume of work involved in an audit of any sizeable social security scheme usually makes an annual external audit an impracticable proposition, without the support of an internal audit.

An *audit* is defined as "the independent examination of, and expression of opinion on, the financial statements of an enterprise/organization by an appointed auditor, in pursuance of that appointment and in compliance with any relevant statutory obligation".

"Internal audit" has been defined as "an independent appraisal activity within an organization for the review of accounting, financial and other operations as a basis of service to management. It is a managerial control which functions by measuring and evaluating the effectiveness of other controls". It exists because of a management decision or, more usually in social security institutions, because of a statutory requirement.

Internal auditors are generally employees of the social security institution. They are, however, independent of the institution by virtue of their authority and the person(s) to whom they report. They should *not* be involved in any part of the operational process.

Internal audit has a vital role to play in the running of a social security institution and embodies a number of important practical advantages:

- from management's point of view, the auditor provides an expert opinion on difficult matters of accounting judgement;

- it helps to ensure that the accounting system, introduced by management to record transactions and safeguard funds, is working properly. If there are significant weaknesses, the auditor will point these out and perhaps suggest ways of improving the system. If there are material errors in the accounts, the auditor will draw management's attention to them so that corrective action can be taken and so that the reason for their occurrence can be investigated. The auditor will draw management's attention to any staff fraud or incompetence discovered in the course of the audit;

- the knowledge that an audit will be carried out helps to deter personnel from risking a fraud;

- those who the institution is there to serve — contributors and beneficiaries — also benefit from the auditor's work. An independent audit not only protects the funds but also lends credibility to the institution's financial statements, and helps protect all those who have an interest in its operations.

Internal auditors would audit:

- the work of offices in connection with the receipt of contributions and the authorization and payment of benefit claims;

- the work of the various sections of the contributions division, in so far as it relates to the collection of contributions, the authorization of benefits and the maintenance of records;

- the work of the staff services division in relation to the cost of administration.

A considerable part of this work will inevitably be carried out in local offices, where the institution has a local office network (or in regional offices, where it does not). Many of the larger social security organizations have more than one team of auditors — usually operating from regional or headquarters offices — each team being responsible for the auditing of a group of offices.

Further comments are appropriate on the independence of the auditors, as follows.

Independence of scope

The scope of the auditor's work should not be restricted. They should be free to examine and report on the activities of any department or part thereof. The decision to include/exclude any area of activity must rest only with the audit manager.

Independence of access

The internal auditor must have an unchallengeable right of access at all reasonable times, without prior notice, to all financial and associated records of the organization, and must be able to require any explanations deemed necessary.

Independence of report

The audit manager should be able to report to all levels of the organization. In most organizations it is desirable that the audit manager's own direct line manager should be either the chief executive or a senior member of top management. This will normally ensure greater independence and substantially enhance the effectiveness of the audit function.

Independence of activity

Auditors should never become involved in the operation of any system which they will ultimately be required to report on. Where auditors *do* become involved in systems and procedures — and unfortunately this is not uncommon — their independence is compromised, and there is a consequential loss in the audit's effectiveness.

Independence of personnel

Where resources are scarce, this can be difficult to achieve. However, audit staff *should* be totally independent of the staff who operate the systems. One practical way of avoiding the problem is to remove or resist the temptation for short-term expedients. For example, a solution to staffing difficulties is sometimes to "borrow" specialist staff to help with peak workloads, but this should be avoided in the case of auditors.

Independence of mind

Whilst impossible to define or measure, this is nevertheless a very important requirement for internal audit personnel. Without it, they may be deflected from their objective.

Many managers and staff are guilty of adopting a negative attitude towards the internal audit function. This is understandable if auditors present themselves — or are perceived — as being motivated only by a drive to find errors and criticize the perpetrators, thus adopting a negative attitude to their work. Whilst fulfilling an independent appraisal function, it should also be recognized by internal auditors that they are one of the tools of management and have a responsibility to provide a service to managers. Such an approach will be seen as positive and constructive and will, hopefully, lead to greater acceptance of their role.

E. Security considerations

The sections dealing with financial controls, internal auditing (earlier in this unit) and the security requirements relating to benefit payments (Module 5, Unit 2) provide general guidance on financial security. Managers have broader responsibilities for security, however, in particular the security of the institution's staff, premises and property. These aspects will be examined in this section.

Managers of any organization have unpalatable facts to consider in connection with security matters. Fire, theft, vandalism, crime, and regrettably even terrorist activities, are as likely to affect social security institutions as any other public or private organization. The institution's organization and management must therefore have regard to, and seek to minimize, such risks.

The ultimate responsibility for the security of the organization's personnel rests with senior management, even though everyone must play their appropriate part in attaining, then maintaining, a satisfactory level of security.

History is littered with examples of organizations which tightened up their security procedures *after* experiencing a major incident. It is much more difficult to tighten it sufficiently so as to *prevent* major incidents.

Larger organizations will expect to have their own in-house security units or specialists; in smaller ones, the chief responsibility for day-to-day security issues may rest with a central services, premises or office services unit. Increasingly, there is a tendency to engage external, specialist security companies, either to advise on or to assist with all or part of the security operation.

At an early stage in the development of the institution's security operations, it will be necessary to assess and identify the risks which need to be safeguarded against. If the institution has its own highly trained security expert, perhaps risk assessment can be made without outside help. If not, local police crime prevention officers are usually very willing to provide advice and guidance. However the assessment is carried out, departmental heads must be fully involved, for they *should* be the ones who are most aware of the problems and risks in their respective area of operation. They should also be heavily involved with the subsequent application and monitoring of agreed security measures, within their own departments, by using methods which will not detract from the department's efficiency.

Managers are, however, inevitably pre occupied with their own main purpose and many therefore view security as an inconvenient and irrelevant distraction from the main operations. There is also a reluctance on the part of some managers to admit that security weaknesses or lapses exist, in case that reflects badly on themselves. Sometimes there is no alternative but to tell individual managers, quite forcefully, that security *is* part and parcel of a manager's job — whether they like it or not!

Fig. 8:
"... managers are ... pre-occupied with their own main purpose ..."

The areas of risk vary considerably from country to country, region to region and indeed city to city, and are too many and various to examine fully. However, it may be useful to refer briefly to some of the more common ones.

- **Office location**
  This may have a bearing on the level of susceptibility to vandalism, theft or pilferage. Additional precautions (fences, doors and window shutters, etc.) might be appropriate. It may be necessary to employ security staff at entrances/exits to monitor and control arrivals and departures.

- **Personal identification**
  Employees may need to wear ID name cards, badges, photographs, to enable security staff to differentiate between members of staff and possible intruders.

- **Security of personal belongings of the staff**
  Staff need somewhere to lock personal valuables — handbag, wallet, briefcase, etc. Small personal lockers are one solution; another option is to ensure that *every* member of staff has (at least) one lockable desk drawer for official items and another lockable one for personal items.

- **Security of records and documents**
  This is a major security consideration. Social security institutions hold vast amounts of confidential information about contributors and beneficiaries. The organization's own personnel records are also highly confidential. The greatest attention must therefore be paid to securing *all* confidential records and documents. Regrettably, it is often true that "familiarity breeds contempt" and many organizations are guilty of a lack of care with records and documents. Staff become so used to handling confidential information that there is a tendency to become blasé about its value and significance. It is not uncommon to find confidential records filed in cupboards or cabinets which, although lockable, always (even overnight) remain *un*locked.

- **Security of cash**
  Money, in whatever form, is the most attractive target for theft. It is almost always unidentifiable, does not need the intervention of a "receiver" and the benefits of stolen money are immediate. Insurance against loss or theft can sometimes be taken out by an organization but this type of insurance is usually expensive. The best form of insurance is to make sure that it cannot be stolen.

  Most organizations make clear to their staff that they will not be held responsible for the loss or theft of personal money from official premises *unless* it is handed over for safe keeping (for example, to the cashier). Any breaches of office rules about leaving money in an insecure place — whether personal or official money — *must* result in the most severe reprimand. Not only does it increase the risk of theft but, as importantly, it places *all* other staff under suspicion if money is stolen.

  Regular reminders are required about the need for maintaining strict security but, unfortunately, these tend to be given only *after* an incident has occurred.

- **Locks and keys**
  The task of controlling locks, keys and key records is any manager's worst nightmare! Yet it has to be done — and done meticulously. It is essential that *all* security keys are signed for (so that key holders can be identified) and that duplicate keys are safely and securely lodged (preferably in an office safe). The training of staff to develop the habit of not releasing keys, or other items of value, without a signature acknowledging receipt, is a vital part of the overall training effort.

- **Fire precautions**
  Fire prevention measures, fire drills and evacuation procedures are ways in which the risk of fires can be reduced and of minimizing the consequences if there is a fire. Advice should be obtained from local fire prevention officers about all aspects of safety precautions.

- **Bomb threats**

  Regrettably, it has become increasingly necessary for many organizations to consider taking precautions against indiscriminate acts of violence and terrorism. The threats and actual risks can take several forms, ranging from malicious or hoax telephone calls to explosive and incendiary devices, and letter bombs. Policies need to be formulated and agreed for dealing with particular contingencies, always giving due consideration and weight to the views and advice of those who will be asked to carry out specific duties, for example, those who will need to search premises for suspicious items.

  Detailed instructions need to be produced for *all* personnel so that everyone knows *exactly* what is required of them in the event of a threat being received, or for the need for full or partial evacuation, or for additional action after such an event. It is always advisable to notify police and fire authorities immediately and, as a matter of good neighbourliness, the occupants of adjoining or nearby buildings should also be told what is happening.

  There are three basic options in bomb threat situations: evacuating and searching before re-entry; searching without evacuation, and ignoring the message. Clearly, many factors have to be considered before deciding which course of action is appropriate and this is why it is essential that plans are prepared in detail which will enable prompt decisions and action to be taken in the event of a threat or explosion.

  There is, of course, no warning where letter bombs are used. This therefore means that the standing arrangements for receipt and opening of postal items *must* have regard to the possibility of such items being received at any time. This necessitates the issue of detailed instructions on the precautions to be taken when handling incoming mail to *all* personnel who are involved in any way in the post opening process.

- **Industrial action**

  Unfortunately, not all industrial action or protests are peaceful and non-violent. Again, therefore, it is wise to lay down plans for any activities which might put the organization's people or premises at risk. There are situations where the police may need to be brought in, and it is therefore essential that any such plans are discussed and agreed with them.

- **Office closures**

  There will be times throughout the year, particularly at holiday periods, when offices are closed for several days. Special arrangements need to be made at such times to ensure a satisfactory level of security during those periods. Also, short days and long hours of darkness present increased opportunities for intruders to steal from or do damage to premises.

The features referred to above are some of the possibilities which should be taken into account when security risks are being anticipated and which must be catered for when the organization is drawing up the various contingency plans.

ADMINISTRATION OF SOCIAL SECURITY

MODULE 2:
COVERAGE AND REGISTRATION

International Labour Office Geneva

MODULE 2

COVERAGE AND REGISTRATION

UNIT 1: Coverage

Introduction

The manual on *SOCIAL SECURITY PRINCIPLES* (No. 1 in this series) deals comprehensively with the issue of coverage, and the topic is not therefore dealt with in detail in this manual.

This unit makes reference only to those aspects of coverage which have a direct bearing on the Module's primary focus, registration.

What is meant by "coverage"?

In the previous Module, reference was made to the definition and the aim of social security. Following from those, it is clear that the ultimate objective must be to provide the protection which social security offers to *all* the people who are likely to be affected by the circumstances — the "nine contingencies" — which the scheme guards against.

The ideal would clearly be to provide social security protection to the *whole* community; in other words, coverage should be truly universal. What is ideal is not, however, always possible to achieve. Even those countries with the most advanced forms of social protection would not claim that *every* individual has complete or adequate coverage. Such schemes are costly and, as a result, benefits are usually low. In reality, coverage of the whole community is extremely difficult to achieve.

In practice, therefore, the nature and extent of social protection will vary significantly, within any given country, between different sections of the population.

The extent of coverage and who is protected

Almost every country has taken a gradualist approach to coverage under the social security scheme and initially many of those who are excluded simply reflect practical considerations. Most countries start by covering those sectors which are reasonably well organized and where individual workers can be readily identified. Often this will have resulted from pressure from specific sectors of the labour force.

The historical pattern of social security schemes has been to cover specific occupational groups initially (e.g. miners, railway employees, etc.) then gradually and progressively extend coverage through other sectors, to more and more people, as the social security organization gains administrative experience. However, the result of such an approach will inevitably be partial and uneven coverage in the initial stages of a scheme's development.

Many new schemes initially include only specific occupational groups or perhaps only workers in the formal urban sector. In addition to this form of limitation, it is also common for schemes to limit coverage to only the larger employers, e.g. those employing more than "x" number of employees — where "x" might be anything from five to a hundred, depending on the country and the scheme. In this way, at the outset, the scheme can reach a substantial proportion of the workforce and then pick up the remainder in later operations as it is extended.

It needs to be pointed out, however, that there are a number of schemes which, despite having been in operation for several years, have still not achieved an extension beyond the *initial* level of coverage. As a result, many of them still exclude:

- employers with less than five workers (for example, Bahrain, Bangladesh, India, Indonesia, Nepal, Pakistan, Saudi Arabia and Sudan);[1]

- or employers with less than ten workers (for example, Iraq, Jordan, Liberia, Myanmar, Nigeria, Uganda);[2]

- domestic workers;

- groups of workers in low-paid employments;

- casual and seasonal workers, etc.

---

1 & 2. All "country information" included in this manual is extracted from: *Social security programs throughout the world*, Social Security Administration, Office of Research and Statistics, USA (SSA Publication No. 13-11805, July 1995).

It should therefore be remembered that, whilst there is often a strong case to be made at the outset for such restrictions, it can become increasingly problematic to take excluded groups on board at a later stage.

In acknowledging that administrative problems *will* result from the inclusion of certain groups of workers, it must also be remembered that restricting coverage for purely administrative reasons is likely to create an imbalance between the "haves and the have-nots", some scheme members being seen as having privileges and protection whilst others are excluded.

Enforcement of the provisions of a scheme becomes more difficult at the points where the limitations are imposed and the interests of those covered also become more difficult to protect. Confusion may arise as to whether the limitation applies in a particular case and this creates opportunities for evasion of liability. Similar problems will also arise over benefit entitlements. All these factors and issues underscore the importance of regularly reviewing and re-appraising the restrictions and limitations embodied in a scheme, with their continuing usefulness and relevance being regularly questioned. On the other hand, it is inadvisable to extend coverage to groups who would be reluctant to participate, or difficult to identify for registration purposes, or with whom compliance/enforcement action would be ineffective.

It quickly becomes apparent that balancing all these competing demands is far from easy, and decisions about limitations and restrictions should not be taken lightly.

Exclusions from coverage

It may be helpful at this point to make reference to particular groups or sectors of the community which are often considered for exclusion from schemes.

Higher-paid employees

Clearly, some employees will always earn far higher wages and salaries than others and, in the early days of insurance-based social security schemes, it was common to find that the higher-paid workers were excluded from coverage. The basis for exclusion was that they were probably less at risk than lower-paid workers and that, in any case, they could better afford to cover themselves by personal insurance.

When flat-rate, contributory schemes were developed, giving the same rate of benefit to each worker, higher-paid workers were usually compulsorily covered. However, they were at the same time at a disadvantage. They paid the same contribution as the majority of workers (because the rate was set at a level which the majority of workers could afford) but this was disproportionately low in relation to the higher-paid worker's wage/salary; when they then became beneficiaries, the flat-rate benefit usually failed to meet their needs.

For this and other reasons, the "earnings-related" system of social security came into being. Under this system, benefits are related to the lost/interrupted earnings of the individual who, when working, pays contributions at a rate which has regard to his earnings level.

It should be noted, however, that earnings-related schemes will often involve a maximum rate of benefit (prescribed in the legislation) and a "ceiling" on contributions (meaning that contributions are paid only up to a prescribed level).

Occupational pension plans

In many countries some of the workers were already covered by different types of sectoral or employer-based pension protection schemes at the time social security measures were being planned and introduced. Such pension arrangements often resulted from trade union pressure. These schemes tended to cover only a limited number of the total labour force and frequently suffered from deficiencies. One major deficiency was the lack of "portability" — the ability to be able to carry pension rights, which were being built up with one employer, with the worker when he moved to another employer on a change of job.

The problem of coordinating existing occupational plans with social security schemes has proved difficult to resolve. On the one hand, the interests of solidarity suggest that all workers, from whatever background, should be members of the social security scheme. On the other hand, some workers do not welcome the idea that they should surrender all or part of what they see as special arrangements which have been hard fought for. Employers have also been known to use the occupational scheme to influence workers to remain in their employment since, if they left, they would lose their pension rights.

Several solutions to these problems have been attempted. They range from letting workers "opt out" of the general scheme, provided they have adequate pension coverage; taking over the occupational funds and their assets and liabilities; or allowing the occupational plan, in a full or revised form, to continue as a supplement to the general social security provisions.

In industrialized countries over recent years there has been a trend towards supplementary (mainly occupational) pension schemes. Official encouragement has often been given for the provision of such supplementary pensions over and above what the general scheme provides. This trend may well be a result of the perceived overall inadequacy of the social security pension and the financial pressures on social security resources.

Government and parastatal workers

Government workers in most countries have, for many years, been covered by their own special — and often comprehensive — protection measures. These are usually established by legislation and typically include, in addition to terms of service and working conditions, the benefits to which they are entitled when they have work accidents, fall sick, become invalids, retire, etc.

Public service pensions and benefits, like the wages and salaries paid to public servants, are almost always paid from public funds. In one sense, these pension plans can be seen as occupational pension plans — operated by the government in its role of employer. In another sense, government workers — because of the nature of their employment — are in a rather special category since, once appointed, they usually continue in that employment for the whole of their working life and can only be dismissed in very special circumstances. There are sound reasons for such an arrangement, not least that it is one way of avoiding political bias against them.

All this means that, when policies are being worked out for developing or expanding a national social security scheme, it is necessary to consider whether to *include* public servants — in the interests of solidarity — or whether to *exclude* them because of their special conditions of work/benefits. This is all the more important in countries where a very large proportion of the working population is engaged in the public service.

Similar considerations may need to be applied to parastatal workers and there are many countries where the legislation relating to their occupational benefits is based on the legislation for government workers.

Rural areas

Social security was first developed to meet the economic needs of urban, industrialized workers. Rural and agricultural workers also have specific and economic needs — in many cases even more so than their urban counterparts — but it has never been easy to extend conventional social security programmes to rural areas.

There is no single, world-wide, uniform model of agriculture. Patterns vary markedly from country to country and region to region and stem from all sorts of local conditions — tradition, soil, systems of land tenure, etc. At one end of the spectrum are large farms, with wage-earning labour and, at the other, tribal lands, subsistence small holdings, share-cropping, seasonal labour, etc. Because of this diversity, "standard" social security programmes have been difficult to develop for this sector and the result is that, in many countries, there is only very limited social protection for rural workers. Indeed, often there is none at all.

In developing countries, it has seldom proved possible to extend protection to the countryside for the reasons mentioned above but also because they are often compounded by poor infrastructure, poor communications and problems of identity.

One approach might be to design special social protection schemes which suit the particular needs of the agricultural sector. This might include providing insurance for crop and natural disasters; better and guaranteed prices; marketing assistance; improved health services; assistance with housing costs, etc.

Family workers

Where members of a family work together in a business undertaking which belongs to the family — or one of the family members — it is usually very difficult to establish whether there is genuine employment of one individual by another, or whether it is a common venture. In such situations it is also difficult to determine contribution liability (in a social insurance scheme) and compensation liability (in occupational injury schemes). There are also great opportunities for collusion in fraudulent benefit claims. For all these reasons, family workers are generally excluded.

Non-national employees

It is rare for non-nationals to be excluded from a scheme solely on nationality grounds. It is more common for schemes to make provision for the exclusion of a non-national who is in the "host country" temporarily *and* who is covered during that period by a scheme in another country (normally, though not necessarily, the country of origin — the "home country") which provides comparable benefits.

The main difficulty usually lies in establishing that the schemes *are* comparable and that the non-national retains equal rights whilst away from the "home country".

Arrangements — widely referred to as reciprocal arrangements — now exist between many countries. These ensure that the rights of contributors are not affected by temporary residence in a "host country". Normally, however, they do *not* exclude the employee from paying contributions in that country. Despite such arrangements, the problems associated with migrant workers are considerable.

The self-employed

The exclusion of the self-employed from schemes, or from parts thereof, is often automatic. Employment injury cover for the self-employed is rare, as is cover for unemployment benefit and workmen's compensation. The reasons for such exclusions often have as much to do with the potential administrative difficulties of inclusion as with any other consideration.

Exclusion of this group from other types of scheme may be because the benefits available cannot be made financially attractive to them. A good example of this is the provident fund, the main attraction of which — for the member — is the fact that the employer also makes a contribution. Without the employer's input, the contributor would receive a very poor return on the contributions which he himself has to pay into the fund.

Similarly, social insurance schemes also rely heavily on employers' contributions — to support the level of benefits. If the self-employed are to be admitted to such schemes, on equal financial terms but paying the *whole* of the contribution shared by employers *and* employees, the rates would not be attractive for them. Schemes which *do* include the self-employed usually require them to pay a lower rate of contribution in recognition of this, but with the level of benefit cover also being reduced.

Where family benefits are still provided on an occupational basis, they too are usually at a lower rate for the self-employed but the general trend is for family benefits to be provided on a universal basis, by the state.

Again, the administrative difficulties need to be taken into account, for it is widely recognized that the tasks associated with record keeping, together with the difficulties of collecting contributions from the self-employed, are often out of all proportion to the amounts they pay into the scheme. For these reasons, developing countries often specifically exclude — or do not attempt to compulsorily include — the self-employed.

The non-employed

For much the same reasons, the inclusion of the non-employed (as distinct from the unemployed) gives rise to similar difficulties. Schemes which do require compulsory membership for the non-employed will generally provide a very limited range of benefit cover, perhaps restricted only to some of the long-term benefits. It is more common for the non-employed to participate as voluntary members.

Voluntary contributors

In an attempt to extend coverage to as wide a selection of the population as possible, a number of countries allow categories of persons who were previously compulsorily insured to become voluntary contributors or, in the case of provident funds, to continue to be members. In this way such people can continue to build up their insurance or provident fund records and subsequently meet the eligibility requirements of the scheme. This provision is sometimes extended to the self-employed — indeed, occasionally to the non-employed — where the scheme has not yet been applied to them.

On the face of it this is commendable but it does raise special difficulties. First, it is not always easy to collect the contributions once an individual has chosen to start paying voluntarily. Second, it is necessary to guard against the payment of contributions, by the voluntary contributor, at an inflated level in order to obtain higher benefits than are appropriate — "benefit-inspired contributions". These are notoriously difficult to prove and control. Third, the arrangements must be carefully monitored to make sure that advantage is not being taken of the scheme by people who are "high risks" and who may adversely affect the prospects of other members.

Statistics

S tatistics on coverage are expressed in a variety of ways, e.g. as a percentage of the labour force; as a percentage of the economically active or as a percentage of the population as a whole.

Periodically the ILO conducts an international survey of social security schemes which includes a questionnaire on financing (receipts and expenditures) and the coverage of schemes. These data are published in **"The cost of social security"**[1] (which contains a series of comparative tables) and the **"Basic tables"**[2] (which contains the data for each country taking part in the survey).

---

1 *The cost of social security: Fourteenth international enquiry, 1987-1989. Comparative tables.* ILO, Geneva, 1996.

2 *The cost of social security: Fourteenth international enquiry, 1987-1989. Basic tables.* ILO, Geneva, 1995.

UNIT 2: Registration

Introduction

In order that liable employers and employees can be brought within the scope of the contribution system, they must be registered with the scheme. It is vital that this first stage, in what will become a long process of collecting and recording contributions and paying benefits, is dealt with thoroughly so as to ensure that sound, accurate, basic records can be established and that contributions can be collected thereafter, as required by the legislation.

Identification of the scheme's participants — workers and employers — is therefore one of the largest and most important tasks of the social security administration.

Is that identification necessary? This clearly depends on the nature of the scheme. In a universal public scheme, where the only test to be satisfied, for receipt of benefits, is nationality and/or residence over a period of time, there is no need for past records to be maintained because the satisfaction of the test can be determined at the time of submission of the benefit claim.

In social insurance schemes, however, where title to benefit depends on qualifying periods in, or contributions paid to, the scheme, it is essential to have up-to-date records which are readily available. In other words, it is necessary to know that an individual is a legitimate participant of the scheme and also to have a record of that participation.

The employer's role in social security schemes is absolutely vital since it is largely through the employer that so much of the scheme is administered.

A. *Registration of employers*

Generally, the identification of employers is not as difficult as the identification of workers. The majority of employers are clearly identifiable enterprises, organizations or individuals. Frequently they will have had to obtain a permit from an appropriate authority — often a central or local government department — before being able to start the business. Numerically there are, of course, far fewer employers than workers and this is a factor which reduces the potential for difficulty with employer registration.

Nevertheless, there are some areas of economic activity where it is not always easy to identify the employer of certain types of worker. The building and construction industries, certain mining and agricultural operations, and those business activities which involve contractors and subcontractors, are just some of the problem areas facing most social security organizations. Problems also arise where scheme members work under a contract *for* service rather than a contract *of* service.

Legislation

These examples illustrate the necessity for ensuring that the legislation defines, as precisely as possible, those who are deemed to be "employers" for the purposes of the scheme. The law will usually also specify the manner and period in which an employer must register and the penalties for failing to do so.

Registration information

The information needed from an employer at the time of registration will usually include: the title of the undertaking; its status under company law and/or the person(s) legally responsible for the undertaking; the type of activity in which it is engaged; relevant address(es); number of employees; perhaps — where the scheme covers employment injury on the basis of rates varying with risk — additional information may also be required so as to determine the class or level of risk.

Whether the employer registration process takes place at the central, regional or local level will depend on many factors, not least the size of the social security institution, the method of collecting and recording contributions, and whether the organization includes regional and/or local tiers. It is desirable, however, that ongoing contact with employers (e.g. for registration of employees, compliance activities, etc.) be maintained at the local level wherever possible, not withstanding that registration documents may be held at the central (or, less commonly, the regional) office.

Employers should also be required to notify any significant changes in the details provided on the original registration document.

It is good practice for an early visit to be made to all newly registered employers, by an inspector of the social security organization, as an educational measure. Such an approach may well save time and prevent problems in the future by resolving any initial difficulties or doubts which the employer is experiencing.

Many schemes issue the employer with a certificate of registration containing, as a minimum, the employer's registration number and the date from which liability commenced. Clearly, there is a need for the social security organization to treat such certificates as security items and to issue them in a controlled way.

When businesses wind up, registration numbers become free but it is *not* a good idea to re-allocate these numbers to new registrants. Old numbers, for terminated employers, should simply remain in the registration indexes (or in a separate — or "dead"- file) for future reference, e.g. in the event of queries arising on contribution or benefit issues for ex-employees of the terminated business.

Unique number

The employer's registration number deserves further mention. The number *must* be unique — in just the same way as with motor vehicle licence numbers — and no two employers may have the same number. The employer should be required to quote the registration number on *all* communications, for it will facilitate not only correct identification but also the many administrative operations relating to contribution remittance, collection, recording, non-compliance activities, etc.

Fig. 9:
"The employer's registration number ...
must be unique ...
no two having the same number ..."

There are two principle methods of numbering. The first is a simple, sequential number; the second is a more complex system combining a sequential serial number *and* a coded prefix or suffix. The coded portion can be used to refer to a geographical area or zone, and/or to the type of industry/service/economic activity, etc. Where a component of the number is used to denote the type of economic activity, it is usually the International Standard Classification (adopted by the Economic and Social Council of the United Nations) which is used.

Supervision of registration

It is essential that the social security organization systematically ensures that *all* liable employers have registered. This task is normally the responsibility of the administration's enforcement inspectorate and inspectors must follow up all leads as to the existence of establishments which have not yet registered. Brief reference has already been made to some of the authorities which may be able to help the social security institution to learn of newly established businesses (local, regional or central licensing authorities; land registries; labour inspectorates, etc.) and maximum use should be made of such organizations. Indeed, formal arrangements can be agreed between them and the social security institution for the one to notify the other when new — or previously unregistered — businesses are identified.

There are many other ways of learning of commencement, change or cessation of business operations, including: systematic examination of official announcements of the formation, amalgamation, liquidation of companies; bankruptcies; complaints from employees (often through their trade unions), etc. It is wise to develop procedures for ensuring that information emanating from such sources can be made available to the social security organization.

Yet another approach, used successfully in a number of countries, is to impose a requirement for an official clearance certificate to be obtained from the social security organization in order to tender for government contracts, or to apply for export licences or for other important commercial operations.

B. Registration of employees — scheme members

Initial registration

In order for any social security scheme to operate effectively and efficiently it is a central requirement that each individual member is allocated a social security reference — or membership — number, and *only one* number. The problems which result from duplicate and multiple registrations of members are enormous and everything possible must be done to avoid them.

Fig. 10:
"... each individual member ... is allocated ... only one number ..."

An effective system demands that all those who are engaged in insurable employment — employment which, under the social security legislation, requires the payment of contributions — *are* properly registered *and* that they retain the *same* social security number throughout the remainder of their lives.

The registration process is usually initiated either by the employer or the employee but there are circumstances in which the social security institution itself may need to initiate the process. The information required from the member, at the time of the initial registration, will clearly vary from one social security organization to another but, as an absolute minimum, it would include:

- full name;
- date of birth;
- place of birth;
- sex;
- address;
- employer's name, address and registration number.

The variety of additional information required by different schemes will depend on a number of factors: whether or not there is an organized, national procedure for the registration of births; how universal, accurate and reliable any such system is; the level of literacy in the country; whether that level varies between urban and rural areas; large numbers of people having the same family names; the extent to which reliable documentary evidence of births, marriages, deaths, etc., is available. It is the presence or absence of such factors which will help to determine the extent of information required at the registration stage.

Additional information may therefore need to include the following:

- the name(s) of parent(s);
- maiden name (for married women);
- national identity card number, if the country has such a system;
- employment book number (if applicable);
- spouse's name(s).

The objective of recording this type of information is simply to avoid duplicate/multiple registrations and, in the event that registrations *are* duplicated, to be able to more easily merge duplicated records. Wherever practicable, the information provided at the initial registration stage should be verified, if possible against official, reliable documentary evidence (birth or baptism certificates, passports, driving licences, marriage certificates, etc.).

Some social security organizations even go so far as to require photographs or thumb/finger print(s) as additional evidence and means of identification.

All the identity information will usually be presented by way of a registration form, completed by the scheme member and - for some schemes — endorsed by the employer.

The importance of prompt registration procedures

It is essential to complete the registration process and to issue the social security number to the new member in the shortest possible time. If this is not done quickly, there is a chance that the employee may move on to another employer and, not having a social security number to give to that employer, begin yet another registration process. This is perhaps the most common cause of duplicate/multiple registrations. It follows, therefore, that the registration process must be simple and speedy. In turn, this means that the information required from the new member, at the registration stage, should be kept to the minimum commensurate with reliable identification. Any advantages of additional means of identification — e.g. photographs or fingerprints — should be carefully weighed against the cost and additional time involved.

It cannot be over-emphasized that the registration process *must* be rapid and accurate. However, it is appreciated that this will often present major difficulties in countries where communications and infrastructure are problematic or where there is ignorance of or opposition to the scheme.

Membership cards

On completion of the registration process, most social security organizations provide the member with some form of identity or membership card. This has then to be produced by the member in support of future benefit claims or when enquiries are made about his records, etc.

Where this type of membership or identity card is used, it is important that be portable and durable and, for this reason, are often issued as a laminated card; some also bear the photograph and/or fingerprint(s) of the member.

An additional advantage of this type of card is that it tends to emphasize its importance to the member, as well as offering a degree of permanency. It may also be useful where the availability of certain benefits depends on immediate identification of the member, for example with medical benefits such as outpatient or emergency treatment at hospitals or clinics. This is one example of a card which may usefully include a photograph.

Some countries issue a small booklet to the member in which to record details of employment, name(s) of employer(s) and sometimes also the details of contributions paid by the member. However, the development of computerized social security systems has increasingly resulted in employment and contribution records being maintained, by the organization, in the form of electronic data. As a consequence, individual booklets, and cards containing adhesive stamps, are increasingly becoming a thing of the past.

Whatever format is chosen, it is most essential that the newly registered member quickly receives some tangible evidence that he *has* registered, which also provides him with his social security number and which emphasizes that he must quote that number each time he contacts the social security organization, for whatever purpose.

The registration number

This will be referred to in different ways in different countries. Terms used will include: social security number; national insurance number; membership number; scheme number; fund number, etc. For ease of reference, the term "social security number" will be used throughout this manual.

The numbering system

The make-up of a social security (registration) number varies enormously from country to country. It may be a simple, sequentially allocated number or it may be a complex number containing, in addition, special combinations of coded numbers and/or letters.

Those coded elements may include or indicate data which is of use to the scheme or to its administrative processes. Examples would include: year of birth; year/locality of initial registration; sex; employer registration number, etc. With computerized systems it is common to include a check digit in the number, so that the computer can detect any coding errors.

It cannot be over-emphasized that the choice of a numbering system is a matter for *very* careful consideration, not least because once introduced it becomes extremely difficult to modify or change the system.

All the administrative processes in which the number will be used should be examined. It is important to keep the number as short as possible, for a number of reasons: for example, it saves staff time whenever the number is written on documents or transcribed between documents; it speeds up the input stage where computerized systems are in use, for employers as well as the social security administration. A short number is also easier for the member to memorize and is therefore more likely to be correctly quoted in support of benefit claims, when enquiries are made to the social security office, or when a new employer asks for it.

At the same time, however, there may be a legitimate need for the social security organization to have a longer, coded number and this will inevitably counteract some of the advantages of shorter numbers which were referred to above. Clearly, the challenge is to strike a balance between the two conflicting demands.

An additional element may also need to be taken into account: the future development of the scheme and the extent to which its' scope and coverage will be extended, particularly if that will result in the need for large numbers of new members to be registered. Additionally, of course, new generations of workers will also join the scheme and they will need to be registered, each of them with a new and unique social security number.

It will have been seen, from this brief reference to some of the potential problems of design, allocation and issue of social security numbers, that it is a crucial part of the organization's administrative arrangements.

It is common practice, in a decentralized social security organization, for the local office level to be responsible for registration procedures but for the central office to allocate batches of registration numbers (for employers and members) to each local office.

Where it is the central office which allocates numbers, it is usually necessary to notify the appropriate local (in some cases the regional) office of the numbers allotted to persons with whom the local office is concerned. This almost always applies to employer registrations though rarely applies to individual member registrations.

C. Self-employed members

All that has been said about the registration of employees applies equally to self-employed members of a scheme. As mentioned previously, self-employed members may not be entitled to as many of the scheme's benefits but, even so, it will normally be just as essential for the organization to maintain a record of their contributions as for employed members. However, the actual process of registration is so similar that persons who initially register as self-employed are not required to register again even if they should later change status and become an employee.

The danger of duplicate or multiple registration is not normally as great with self-employed members but this does not mean that any less care should be taken with registration procedures, that any less information will be required from the individual, or that the process of registration is any the less urgent or important.

Perhaps the major problem with self-employed members, in a scheme where they are compulsorily included under the legislation, is that of evading registration. This is more common with one-man operations, or very small businesses employing only one or two workers, because that type of business can "hide" more easily and therefore is often harder to discover or locate.

There are other problems associated with the self-employed member, particularly in respect of compliance, but the registration process rarely needs to be any different than for employees. It should be remembered that, once registered, self-employed members will retain the same social security number throughout the rest of their lives. It will *not* be changed, no matter how the employment status may change.

D. Registration of dependants

Bearing in mind that each member of a social security scheme is likely, at some point, to have one or usually more dependants, it is apparent that the task of registering *all* dependants would be a formidable one. It is, of course, possible to include a record of dependants at the registration stage, *if* the social security organization can afford to devote sufficient staff resources to the task. At later stages, however, updates will almost certainly be required to monitor any change in status of those in the dependant categories; this will also cause further demands on staff resources.

It needs to be realized that the cost of maintaining an up-to-date record of dependants is very demanding of staff resources, and is therefore expensive. Judgements must therefore be made about the need for dependants' records and weighed against the cost involved, the value, and the potential use of the stored information.

It is possible to devise systems which provide appropriate cash benefits or health care to dependants but which do not call for detailed and precisely maintained records. Although such systems may carry a degree of risk (for example, of incorrect benefit awards) the administrative savings might well outweigh the small risks involved.

A further factor to be taken into account is whether the social security contribution collection agency really requires dependancy details at the registration stage. The answer is most probably not.

A look at social security systems around the world reveals that offices administering cash benefits do not usually concern themselves with details of dependants until and unless a benefit claim, in respect of those dependants, is actually made.

Experience also shows that the registration of dependants should not be undertaken simply as a matter of course. There must be very compelling reasons — and a real need — before an organization goes down that particular road.

E. Registration records

Records relating to employers

An earlier unit pointed out that the social security institution may well retain records of employers at two levels — local and central. The records will usually consist of at least two indexes, one alphabetical, one numerical (based on employer registration numbers). In this way it is possible to quickly identify an employer's registration number from the alphabetical index, or the name of the employer from the numerical index.

Fig. 11:
*"Records ... consist of at least two indexes ...
alphabetical and numerical ..."*

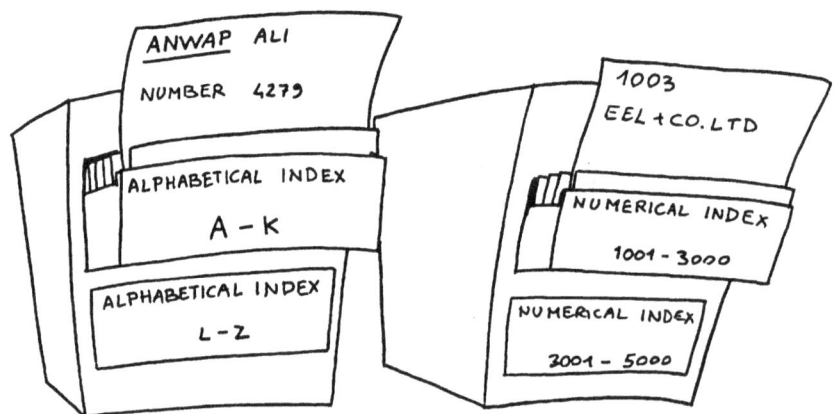

Where computerized systems are in operation, the record can usually be accessed through *either* the name or the number. Even in this case, however, it is often useful to retain some form of manual system, at the local level, to assist the task of monitoring and controlling compliance activities.

Some organizations also maintain auxiliary indexes according to geographical area, address, economic activity, size, or employment sector (e.g. public or private sector).

The basic registers will generally include two main components: the first containing constant information (registration details — name, address, registration number, economic activity, etc.) and the second containing variable information (details of employees, contributions due and paid, etc.).

Control over remittances by employers is exercised from that part of the register containing variable information and when the monitoring of payment/non-payment of contributions is examined (in Module 3) it will be seen that it is the variable information records which are of greatest use.

Records relating to the insured members

The records for scheme members are inevitably of the constant type, as all the information therein will have a relevance to benefit claims activity. The contents will include all the information provided at the initial registration stage and thereafter will be added details of all contributions paid into the scheme.

Organizations which still depend on manual records often maintain both alphabetical and numerical (based on registration numbers) indexes. Computerized systems are generally accessible by using *either* the member's name or number.

The major difference between employer and member registration records is that, whilst it is usually essential for some records relating to employers to be held at the local level, this is rarely the case for individual members.

Each application for registration will need to be checked against the index of insured members *before* a number is allocated. Ideally, this should be done through computerized searches but an initial scrutiny should reveal whether or not the applicant is likely to have been previously registered. The time and effort taken to check a registration will need to be balanced against delays in the allocation of a number and against the consequences of failure or delays in recording the payments of contributions. However, failure to discover any previous registration number will lead to duplicate/multiple registration and, therefore, to untold problems in the future.

ADMINISTRATION OF SOCIAL SECURITY

MODULE 3:
COLLECTION AND RECORDING
OF CONTRIBUTIONS

International Labour Office Geneva

MODULE CONTENTS

UNIT 1: Collection

    A. Structure of the contribution system

    B. Methods of payment and collection systems

    C. Processing contribution payments and monitoring non-payment

    D. Late payment penalties

UNIT 2: Recording

    A. The need for records

    B. The nature of records

    C. Computerization

    D. Employer records

    E. Non-compliance records

    F. Members' records

    G. Centralized and decentralized records

    H. Storage and destruction of records

MODULE 3

COLLECTION AND RECORDING OF CONTRIBUTIONS

UNIT 1: Collection

Introduction

In a contributory social security scheme, the system of collection of contributions is of critical importance. Contributions are the means by which the social security scheme obtains the financial resources on which it depends.

The administration of the collection system often constitutes the largest block of work in the social security organization. The guiding principle in setting up that collection system — from the viewpoint of the both the scheme and its contributors — must be simplicity of administration.

Sometimes there are serious problems in enforcing the legislation and in coping with the workload resulting from collection. These problems tend to become more prevalent as schemes expand into new areas and sectors of the economy (e.g. to smaller employers).

If adequate levels of effectiveness and efficiency in collection are not attained, the repercussions will inevitably be felt across the organization — not least in the processing of benefit claims, where those claims are dependant on contribution records.

Consequently, it is vital that all social security organizations pay close attention to their collection and recording systems.

A. *Structure of the contribution system*

Social security programmes involve the transfer of funds in the form of cash benefits or services. In centrally organized contributory schemes, a financial plan has to be carefully devised to meet projected benefit and administrative expenditures. The financing is established through social security legislation which specifies who must participate in the financing (the contributors to the scheme) and the amounts they must pay (viz. the contribution rates).

In the majority of schemes, the "employing establishments" (the employers) and the "eligible workers" (the insured members) are required to contribute — though not always in equal parts. The employer is responsible for collection (from the employee) and for the remittance of the total contribution (employee's *and* employer's shares, combined) to the social security institution*.

There are various methods of contribution collection because there is a variety of types of contributor, ranging from the very small business, operated by a self-employed individual, to very large companies which have computerized systems for their payroll and social security operations.

Types of contribution

An earlier section made brief reference to the types of contribution systems operating in social security schemes. It is appropriate to look at these in more detail before moving on to payment and collection arrangements.

Flat-rate contribution

The uniform, or flat-rate, contribution system is one in which a fixed amount is paid by contributors, regardless of their earnings level. Although a scheme operating flat-rate contributions may have several different contribution rates (for example, different for young persons than for adults, for males than for females, etc.) within *each* category the amount of the contribution will be uniform, flat-rate, and not related to the individual's earnings.

---

*Where there is also an employment injury scheme in operation, organized separately from the social security scheme, the employers covered by that legislation are usually solely responsible for financing the scheme; thus only the employer is liable for a contribution. Moreover, because these benefits are not usually subject to contribution tests, the collection system is often a simplified one.

Earnings-related contribution

More often, however, the rate paid will be related to the individual's level of earnings, i.e. an earnings-related scheme. In such schemes, contributions are fixed using a simple percentage calculation. Some earnings-related schemes exclude earnings below a certain amount (referred to as "the contribution threshold") and above a certain level (referred to as "the contributions ceiling"). Others may have regard to *all* the earnings when applying the percentage calculation but may also stipulate a maximum total amount of contribution to be paid.

Fig. 12:
" ... Flat-rate and earnings-related schemes ..."

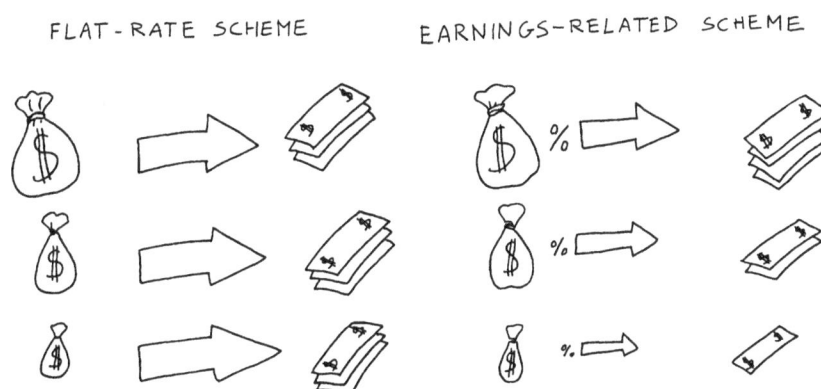

FLAT-RATE SCHEME   EARNINGS-RELATED SCHEME

Wage classes

Yet another approach is that of wage classes, under which there are a number of wage bands, for each of which a specific contribution amount is payable.

Table 1: An illustration of a wage class system

Wage Class	Earnings	Assumed wage	Contribution
1	0 -50	40	4
2	51- 100	70	7
3	101-150	120	12
4	151-200	180	18
and so on, until ...	... any contribution ...	... ceiling is..	... met.

Wage classes simplify a manual contribution system since only a limited number of fixed rates are used. Wage classes can also be used as an instrument to promote redistribution of resources amongst the members of the scheme; this is done by adjusting the amounts due from the lower- and higher-paid workers.

The system can also be appropriate to the self-employed, where earnings are often extremely difficult to assess and verify.

Special rates of contribution

Some countries levy special rates of contribution, for example in certain industries or in certain sizes of establishment. In employment injury schemes, contribution rates may also vary from one industry to another, according to the different levels of risk.

In all of these systems, the contribution will normally be bi-partite (combined worker/employer payments) and may be of equal parts, though often the employer's share will be the greater of the two. In some schemes the very lowly paid worker will pay nothing at all, or perhaps a much reduced rate, sometimes with the employer paying a proportionately higher contribution.

Individual contributors

For individual contributors — for example self-employed or non-employed people — the systems may be similar to those described above, i.e. flat-rate or on a percentage basis. However, it is desirable to make the system for these contributors as simple as possible in order to minimize compliance problems.

Government subsidy

Where a social security programme is subsidized by the government, the additional finance is paid directly into the fund, not through a contribution collection system.

Pay-as-you-earn arrangements

In countries which operate efficient pay-as-you-earn (PAYE) income tax collection systems, and which also have social security systems covering most of the people liable to pay tax, the collection of contributions may be handled by the tax authority as a part of their collection procedures.

Potentially, this is an efficient and cost-effective means of collecting social security contributions and, from the employer's point of view, results in only one remittance for the two organizations and usually requires only one combined set of documents to support the remittances.

Some would argue that this arrangement has the disadvantage of confusing social security and income tax in the minds of contributors, or that it might prejudice the financial autonomy of the social security system, but it operates successfully in some countries (for example in the United Kingdom).

B. Methods of payment and collection systems

In almost all schemes, employees' contributions are deducted from wages/salaries and then paid over, together with employers' contributions, to the social security institution.

Stamp cards

Although a brief explanation of the stamp card method of payment follows, it must be said that this has generally been abandoned, except in the case of some special flat-rate schemes, and has given way to other methods.

The system requires that the employer holds a card for each individual employee and regularly affixes adhesive stamps to the card. Each stamp, affixed either weekly or monthly according to the particular scheme or system, represents and is to the value of the amount of the contribution payable. Stamps are purchased from the social security institution or, more commonly, through the post office. Cards are current for one year, at the end of which, when full, they are exchanged for new ones. The old, "full", cards are then used as posting documents to bring up to date the central records of each contributor.

The method was originally devised for schemes which gave flat-rate benefits for flat-rate contributions and it is not easily adaptable to the collection of wage-related contributions from monthly payrolls.

Payroll system of collection

There are two basic components of the payroll system of contribution payment and collection:

- regular payments of contributions by employers (usually monthly) remitted to the social security institution;

- periodic submission, by employers, of contribution rolls or lists of scheme members — often referred to as "contribution schedules".

Schedules inevitably vary in format but must provide the essential information, which will usually be:

- employer's name, registration number, address;

- period covered by the schedule;

- for each employee:
  social security number, name(s), earnings, contribution deducted;

- dates of commencement/termination of "starters and leavers" during the period covered by the schedule;

- employer's contribution in respect of each employee where necessary (e.g. because of varying rate contribution systems, wage class, special rates for low-paid workers, etc.);

- sub-totals, for each page, grand totals of employee and employer contributions (and possibly of earnings totals);

- a certificate of accuracy by an authorized representative of the employer.

It is usual for the employer to retain a copy of the schedule and for a copy to be sent to the social security institution. Some social security institutions also require a second copy for a decentralized office (e.g. a local office) where it may be needed in connection with compliance activities or benefit claims procedures.

It should be remembered that the data contained on these schedules is the basic, constant, information used for determining members' entitlement to benefits. Schedules therefore have to be stored — and for long periods. Moreover, they need to be stored in a manner which permits easy reference to them, particularly with manually operated systems. Storage methods vary greatly. Some institutions keep microfilm copies. Those submitted in computer readable form (tape, diskette, etc.) must also be safely stored, with precautions taken to prevent "wiping".

The administration *must* establish a policy for retention of basic data. That policy may also need to take account of the country's legal requirements with respect to the period for which basic data must be retained.

Payment method for the payroll system

Under the payroll system, schedule payment system employers pay money at regular intervals to the social security office, in cash, by cheque or through bank transfers. The frequency of remittance to the institution is generally monthly, as most workers are paid monthly. However, even where workers are paid weekly or bi-weekly, the remittance from the employer will still normally be monthly. That remittance will represent the total contributions from *all* workers listed on the schedule *plus* the employer's total contribution for *all* workers.

Although it is usual to require monthly remittances, it is often only necessary for the employer to submit the completed schedules quarterly, or even twice-yearly for some schemes.

Whatever the interval between schedules, the social security administration must reconcile all remittances from the employer with the entries on the schedule(s). The aim must clearly be to ensure that the payment(s) actually *received* by the institution represents the *total* amount of contributions actually *due* — i.e. the contribution liability.

Design of contribution schedules

The increasing use of computerized systems has given rise to a variety of schedule formats, some of them very highly specialized in relation to a particular employer or to the social security institution's administration.

The simplest schedules are pre-printed forms, issued by the social security office, on which the employer manually records all the information. The most sophisticated versions are computer-produced diskettes, prepared by the social security institution and issued to the employer, who then uses his in-house computer system to add the contribution payment details, starters and leavers, changes, etc., before returning the diskette to the institution. There, the information is transferred directly from diskette to member accounts; the record of employer remittances is updated, reconciliation takes place — all via the computerized systems.

In between those two ends of the spectrum will be found a variety of systems, all of which are modifications of the basic payroll method. An increasingly common practice, helpful to both the social security institution and the employer (particularly the employer who is not computerized) is for the institution to pre-print the social security numbers and names on the schedules (based on data taken from the previous schedule) before issuing them to employers. This clearly assists the employer, who only has to add pay and contribution figures and starters/leavers. It also saves time for the institution because it reduces the volume of handwritten data which needs to be keyed into the computer when the schedule is returned by the employer.

An extension of this practice is to pre-print wage/salary and contribution figures also, where these are reasonably static. The employer then only needs to modify the pre-printed schedule to show any changes in the current reporting period.

Which method?

There is no reason why various methods cannot be used concurrently. Indeed, there are advantages in utilizing a variety of payment and collection systems, each of which meet the needs of different groups of employers.

Clearly it will be beneficial for the social security institution to work closely with those employers who have advanced computerized payroll systems. Procedures can then be developed which meet the needs of each party and save time for both. At the same time, there will always be small employers who do not have computer facilities, and the institution will need to use simplified systems for that group.

Even though the references and illustrations above are not exhaustive, it will be apparent that there is a wide variety of contribution payment methods and collection systems. Some of these are imaginative and may look particularly attractive to institutions which, although still using manual systems, are looking to adopt the most advanced systems available.

It should be remembered, however, that social security planners need to have regard to many factors before constructing — or indeed modifying — their procedures for collection of contributions. These include: the information required for the qualifying conditions for benefits; how quickly that information needs to be accessed at the time of the claim;

whether contributions data should be held at central or local levels — or both. Other considerations may also be relevant: certain procedures may be more appropriate where the government is the largest employer; others may be demanded to suit large private employers with their own specialized payroll systems; yet others may be appropriate where employment is geographically widely spread and in small pockets. The extent of the development of infrastructure, communications, banking systems, money transfer facilities, etc., will also have a major influence on payment and collection systems.

In the final analysis, the choice of a collection system is always a matter of balancing the respective interests of employers *and* the social security administration. If there is an agreed preference, the choice will be simple. If not, every effort must be made to meet the wishes of the employers, since it is they who can so easily prejudice the social security operation if a system is imposed on them which, for whatever reason, they dislike.

C. Processing contribution payments and monitoring non-payment

Organization of contributions work

In a typical social security organization, one of the main components to be found at each level of the organization — whether local, regional or central — is a unit dealing with contributions. At the local office level it is generally referred to as the Contributions Section and at regional and central levels as the Contributions Branch or Division.

In administrations which operate on three tiers (see Module 1, Unit 2) it will usually be local offices which are responsible for all day-to-day matters relating to contributions (for their own geographical areas) i.e. registration (employers and employees), collection, inspection, compliance, insurability and liability questions, and enforcement of the legislation. In two-tier organizations, it will generally be the regional office which is responsible.

In the three-tier organization, the regional Contributions Branch will usually be more concerned with oversight, monitoring and control of local office activities and will usually also have an advisory function, giving advice and interpretation to local offices in cases of difficulty.

At the central level, in addition to having overall responsibility for all matters relating to contributions, there will usually be a separate section which has responsibility for the processing and recording of contributions data received from the local level.

The developments in computerized systems of processing and recording contributions data has enabled many social security institutions to install "on-line" electronic data processing (EDP) transmission and retrieval systems. Where such systems are fully networked — i.e. where they can be accessed by any of the administration's offices (local, regional or central) — it has facilitated the decentralization of the processing of contribution schedules. The result is that local offices can input the contributions data directly into the central data base.

Time limits for payment of contributions

The social security legislation should stipulate that the contribution payments — together with the supporting schedules — must be delivered to the social security organization within a prescribed number of days after each calendar month end. This time limit is commonly set at 15 days and, where payment is made later, a penalty will automatically be imposed.

Some employers may pay within the prescribed period but fail to deliver the supporting documents; procedures must be developed to ensure that complications of this sort are prevented. This is one of several reasons for having control systems, operated at the local level, for ensuring prompt and accurate payment of contributions by employers.

Control systems

As schedules and remittances are received by the local office, if dates of receipt are registered, it will be apparent by the payment deadline which employers have failed to submit payments and schedules. Follow-up action may range from a standard postal reminder in cases of isolated late payments, or a visit by the social security inspector, to more serious action if, over a period of time, it has become apparent that an employer is a persistent and regular defaulter. The question of enforcement and compliance will be examined in greater detail in the next module.

Payment methods

The schedules submitted by employers should be accompanied by the supporting payment. This may be received in cash, by cheque, or by a bank receipt where bank transfer is being used. Where the social security institution permits payment to be made to its offices in cash, it is vital that secure procedures are followed in order to prevent internal fraud or abuse, or complicity between social security staff and employers. Payments by cash or cheque should *always* be acknowledged immediately through the issue of official receipts, which must at all times be treated as valuable security items and subjected to tight management controls.

This aspect of social security administration is perhaps the most vulnerable of all its operations and most open to the risk of abuse. Many institutions forbid staff, particularly outdoor staff such as inspectors, to receive or handle cash. It is sometimes difficult, when faced with an employer who has been reluctant to pay his contribution remittance, to decline the offer of an immediate cash payment. At the same time, however, it has often proved too tempting for officers, who are presented with large sums of money, to divert some for their own purposes.

It cannot be over-emphasized how essential it is for the social security organization to devise and implement secure procedures for receipt of monies — and stringently enforce them.

Reconciling payments and schedules

It must not be assumed that the payment made by an employer is correct, that it matches the information on the schedules, or that the correct deductions have been made. It is therefore usual for the contributions section to undertake some form of comparison and reconciliation between the payment and the supporting schedules, along with a check of individual schedule entries. This check may be full or partial, according to the reliability and accuracy of the employer, as revealed by the previous compliance history.

Reconciliation and checking

It is not intended that this manual should provide detailed information or guidance about the checking and reconciliation procedures to be used for payments and schedules. However, it is important that checking and reconciliation *are* carried out — and very soon after they are received — so that queries can be taken up promptly with the employer. The aim must be to complete the check, clear any enquiries and bring individual worker's contributions to account as quickly as possible.

The reconciliation procedures are always important but particularly so in cases where employers — usually the larger ones — remit monthly, at a regular, fixed amount but only submit detailed schedules at three (or even six) monthly intervals. The monthly payments may be seen as a "deposit" and represent the contribution liability for the past month. The submission of the quarterly (or half-yearly) schedule must be accompanied by any adjusting payment which is appropriate.

Internal checks

The checking which takes place in the social security office, most commonly at the local level, will usually focus on verification of

- accuracy of particulars relating to the employer;

- accuracy of data relating to individual employees;

- amounts of wages/salary, periods of employment and their relationship and credibility;

- accuracy of the contribution deduction(s) — where possible to ascertain the appropriate amount;

- arithmetical accuracy of the compilation of the schedule;

- the appropriate amount of money, in respect of contributions and any penalty payments, having been brought to account in the scheme.

External checks

These are the checks performed on the employer's premises and the primary aim is to determine the contribution liability of the employer and ensure that he has discharged this responsibility by paying the appropriate amounts at the correct time. Furthermore, it is necessary to examine wage and other records in order to be satisfied that the employer has included *all* his employees on schedules; a common device is to exclude part of the workforce and thus "under-pay". This is sometimes compounded by the employer deducting contributions from workers but not remitting to the social security office. Checks should also compare *actual* wage/salary payments against those recorded on schedules. Sometimes employers pay more to the worker than the schedule indicates, in order to reduce the contribution liability.

From these few examples, it will be appreciated that there is not only extensive scope for employers to make genuine errors on schedules but also to deliberately provide wrong information or omit it altogether.

External checks should also be made by the organization's inspectors

• as surprise checks, without prior warning, to employers;

• whenever there is a suspicion that "something is wrong";

• when frequent errors are made with schedules or remittances;

• when an employer is regularly late in remitting payments and/or schedules.

D. Late payment penalties

It is common practice, in social security institutions to include in the legislation the right of the scheme's administrators to impose fines if contributions are paid late or not paid at all. Such fines are usually fixed penalties, often at a specific percentage of the amount outstanding each month, and on a cumulative basis.

It is important that the level of fine is carefully chosen. If the employer can earn more in interest, by keeping contribution monies in his bank, than the fine he will ultimately pay, the penalty will have no impact. The aim is to use penalties for late/non-payment primarily as a deterrent, for it is not in the administration's interest to have large numbers of employers who regularly fail to comply — even if additional revenues by way of fines (relatively small amounts at that) are being collected. Penalties therefore need to be sufficiently harsh to "encourage" timely remittance of contributions.

Schemes which do not have penalties built into the legislation are the weaker for it. Enforcement is difficult enough without making it even more difficult by ignoring the need for non-compliance penalties.

UNIT 2: Recording

A. The need for records

It will have become apparent that the success of a social security organization, and whether it meets the needs of the people it was established to serve, depends to a very large extent on the effectiveness of its record keeping and record maintenance.

All social security schemes, whether of the social insurance or provident fund types, *must* identify their members and ensure that their contributions are properly brought to account in the institution's records. Those records usually consist — as a minimum — of individual records of contributions paid, and alphabetical indexes of members, to assist with identification and prevent duplicate accounts. As a valuable by-product, they also provide statistical data of the insured population.

The records are an essential feature of those social insurance schemes which provide old-age or retirement pensions based on earnings over a working life. These are the records which will ultimately show whether an insured member qualifies for a pension and, in earnings-related schemes, the records will provide details of the years of service and earnings data on which the pension will be calculated.

The responsibility for accurate maintenance of the records rests with the social security organization. However, many institutions periodically seek the insured person's verification of the validity of the current records. It should never be left to the member to produce his employment or contributions history data and have to persuade the social security organization that benefit or pension of a certain amount is to be paid. The onus for maintaining such data rests firmly with the organization.

At this point it is useful to remember that, for the vast majority of members, the only personal contact they will have with the institution will be at the time when a benefit is claimed. So far as individual members are concerned, the credibility of the scheme depends on the quality of service received at that point in time and the efficiency and accuracy of that service. This, in turn, depends on whether the scheme maintains accurate and up-to-date records which can be retrieved quickly.

As already mentioned, the development of EDP techniques, the application of information technology and computerized systems, have greatly improved the record-keeping ability of many social security organizations. It must always be remembered, however, that such systems are only as good as the people who design and operate them. The installation of computerized systems does not, of itself, guarantee trouble-free record keeping.

Fig. 13:
"... computerized systems ... have greatly improved ... record-keeping ability ..."

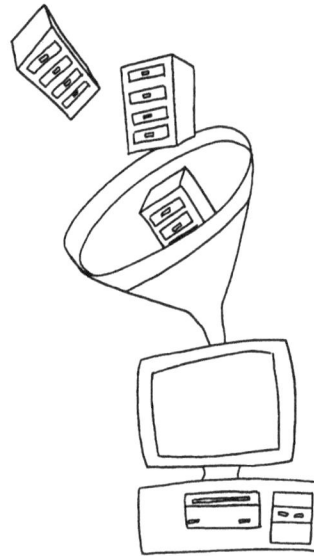

B. The nature of records

It is not possible to provide a standardized plan or a precise model for record keeping, whether for contributions records or any other purposes. As with all other aspects of social security administration, these will vary greatly from scheme to scheme. However, whilst there is no one model, it is possible to identify the *types* of record required and to give some guidelines. At the same time, it should be remembered that the provisions of a particular scheme and the country characteristics must always be taken into account.

Looking beyond the immediate issue of contribution records, the creation and maintenance of any form of records, on the scale required by social security schemes, occupies a great deal of staff time and therefore takes up a substantial proportion of the administrative expense. The high cost of record keeping therefore deserves, and demands, special attention from administrators, who must always be concerned with an increase in efficiency whilst at the same time trying to control — and ideally to reduce — costs.

Prime records

From the administrative point of view, a social security scheme has certain basic record-keeping requirements and obligations, including:

- registration of participants (insured members) and their employers, and their continuing identification throughout the lifetime of the scheme;

- maintenance of employers' records of contributions due and paid;

- maintenance and retrieval of the work history, or record of contributions paid, of the participants;

- maintenance of records of benefit claims;

- maintenance of financial and administrative records for management, auditing and accounting of the scheme;

- (for some schemes) registration of dependants of the scheme members.

These types of document are referred to as *'prime records'*, so called because they are fundamental and vital to the administration and operation of the scheme and are constantly in need of updating with information from *'source records'*.

Prime records are also normally required in perpetuity, destroyed only when a suitable length of time has elapsed following the death of a member. Some prime records may have a valuable temporary purpose but need to be replaced periodically by new, updated material.

Source records

Source records are valuable temporary records from which material has to be extracted and transferred to prime records. Afterwards they may usually be destroyed, unless required for back-up reasons.

A good example of a prime record is the participant's work history or record of contributions. Information and data is transferred to it from source documents, for example from the initial registration form or, on a continuing basis, from employer contribution/payroll schedules. Whilst those schedules will *initially* be prime records, once the data is transferred to the participant's individual work/contribution record, they then become source documents. Schedules are, however, a good example of documents which are often retained for back-up purposes in the event of a future query on the accuracy of the prime records.

One major potential problem with prime records is that of bulk and storage. It is important that security measures are taken to ensure their confidentiality and inviolability. There is an even greater — and potentially more serious — build up of material from source records, even where much thought has gone into the design, standardization and reduction in the size of forms and to the associated storage arrangements.

Some records need to be retained to satisfy legal requirements (e.g. initial registration documents) and, if so, the storage, subsequent retrieval, and protection of such documents can become problematic.

It must be appreciated that the entire administration, with its multifaceted requirements, needs access to different types of information. Hence, benefit information and records are needed, accounts records have to be maintained, medical care documents may need to be set up and preserved, etc.

Additionally, statistical requirements have to be met and data made available for actuarial valuations. The introduction of EDP systems usually means that separate records for each of these operations no longer need to be maintained as each administrative unit can call on data from the central processing unit.

C. Computerization

Social security computerized systems have developed rapidly, over recent years, in order to keep pace with the ever-growing need to handle vast quantities of data and information. Data and information which previously had to be dealt with manually can now be recorded, processed, stored and retrieved much more quickly.

It is necessary to distinguish between data and information and to include at this point a brief comment on data processing. All modern organizations, in common with social security institutions, have certain administrative tasks which need to be carried out to enable them to meet their objectives.

Common features emerge throughout organizations, e.g. the need to:

- collect data and maintain accurate records or files;

- sort, merge and tabulate the records in the files;

- carry out basic calculations;

- handle large volumes of data; and to perform routine and repetitive manipulation of records.

Collectively, these features are referred to as *data processing*. The term can, of course, be applied whether the operations are performed manually or by computer and data processing can therefore be described as "the organizing of and techniques for the collection, processing, storage and output of data". The data which is collected can also be used to produce information. *Stored data*, when combined with *input data* and processed, results in *information*.

For example, if the *stored data* is the rate per hour paid to a labourer, that can then be combined with the number of hours worked — input data — to produce the daily/weekly wage which the labourer should receive; i.e. the *information*. This information can, in turn, be used as input data for further calculations to produce further information.

In addition to *calculating* from data, a data processing system will also involve the *manipulation* of data — sorting, merging and tabulating — to produce *information*.

It follows that, for social security organizations, data processing through computerized systems has great potential for recording, storing, processing contributions data and information, and for using that information in the calculation of benefit awards and payments. This applies particularly with contribution records which involve the recording and storage of data and information about contributions paid over a working lifetime — as long as 50 years or more for some schemes.

Computerized systems are usually very refined and most are programmed with built-in checks which will "question" the input data. For example, with earnings-related contributions, systems will usually be programmed to reconcile contribution payments with wage/salary figures and identify underpaid or overpaid contributions, often with tolerance factors built in. In addition to the reconciliation of individual contributor data, programmes are also able to reconcile total employer remittances with aggregated individual deductions. This facility, to build into the programme a variety of checks and balances, makes it difficult — indeed should make it virtually impossible — to input incorrect data.

Despite the many obvious advantages and benefits which flow from computerized systems, it has to be acknowledged that there are also limitations. Programming — the process of identifying procedures, developing rules and producing them in a form which the computer can understand — requires considerable time and effort and can only be performed by specialized personnel.

Furthermore, the necessity for rigid rules often leads to inflexibility. If there are changes in procedures, computer programmes need to be rewritten, input to the computer and translated into the computer's own internal code. Since data is always handled in accordance with the rules, the computer cannot make exceptions to those rules in the same way that a human can; the result is that sometimes the output can appear nonsensical.

The advances made in fully networked computer systems, i.e. having all offices — local, central and possibly also regional —

connected up to the central data base, potentially extends the availability of access to the system to all the organization's staff. However, it also means that systems must not only be well programmed, in order to prevent erroneous inputs, but also secure enough to prevent abuse of the system.

From this brief reference to the possibilities opened up by electronic data processing, it can be seen how far some systems have moved on from manual, very labour-intensive, methods. It will also be apparent, however, that this is a very specialized area of administration which requires great expertise and detailed planning if it is to enhance the efficiency and effectiveness of the organization to the maximum extent possible.

D. Employer records

Essentially, there are three main types of employer record (already referred to briefly in Module 2, Unit 2E); they are *Indexes, Basic Registers* and *Non-compliance records.*

Indexes

Normally there are two types of index:

- alphabetical;

- numerical — based on employers' registration numbers.

Occasionally an auxiliary one will be used, according to geographical area or address, economic activity, or size of business.

Basic registers

Also referred to previously, these are the records containing constant information (registration details, etc.) and variable information (employees, contributions paid, etc.). The third type of employer record, the non-compliance record, deserves separate mention and is dealt with in the following section.

E. Non-compliance records

These are the records which enable the social security organization to pursue payment from those employers who fail to remit contribution payments by the due date. The records are normally retained and maintained at the office dealing directly with the employer and, in many organizations, this will be at the local level.

Employer files

Two kinds of record are usually necessary. First, a file for each and every employer, on which to retain all documents relating to action taken by inspectorate staff. The file would include reports of interviews, details and records of surprise visits and routine inspections by inspectorate staff, letters and other correspondence, records of telephone communications, etc. This file is therefore a "running record" of all the organization's contacts with the employer. If non-compliance should reach the stage where the employer is prosecuted, it is usual to set up a sub-file on which all the prosecution action and activities are documented. (Prosecution issues are dealt with in detail in Module 4).

Survey cards

The second type of record is a summary file, for each employer, on which is briefly recorded all non-compliance action taken, together with records of inspections and the results of those inspections. This will often be in the form of a card index — often referred to as a "survey card" — and is a ready reference for the inspector when the employer's compliance record needs to be quickly ascertained. The survey card is also useful as a basis for organizing surprise inspections and many institutions also make use of the card index to keep track of employer remittances. For example, as a remittance is received from an employer, his index card is removed from the main run and "put to the back" — still in alphabetical order. As payments are received from employers, their cards are also "filed behind" and it is then apparent which employers have failed to remit by the due date because it is their survey cards which still remain in the main run at that date.

Several times throughout this manual it has been pointed out that "there is no single, standard, system" for each aspect of social security administration. Nevertheless, most systems are variations of the same theme. In the compliance field, systems should serve one main objective — the collection of all due contributions by the due date. Whatever system is adopted, it must have been designed and developed with that specific objective in mind. It also helps if systems are kept simple, particularly manually operated ones, as with the examples given above. Complex procedures are often at risk of not being understood or of breaking down and, if this results in some employers evading payment without being found out, the procedures are clearly meaningless. It should also be remembered that, if this happens, it is likely to result in non-entitlement to benefits by scheme members who work for the defaulting employers.

F. Members' records

Where a social security scheme is based on the universal approach, and where benefits are available to the whole population without contribution tests, there is no need to maintain records of contributions paid by individuals. Nor is it necessary to do so if, for example, a scheme covers only short-term benefits (such as sickness and maternity) and the cash benefits payable under the scheme are based on wages received or contributions paid over a brief, recent period. In such schemes, there is no need to keep individual records covering the whole period of an individual's scheme participation; it is usually sufficient to make enquiries about recent wages or contributions at the time a benefit claim is made.

The situation is very different, however, for schemes which provide long-term benefits such as old-age, survivors, or invalidity pensions. Qualifying periods of contributions are usually spread over many years, perhaps even over an entire insurance lifetime. In these circumstances, it is necessary for the administering authority (normally the social security organization) to keep individual records of *all* contributions paid by *each* insured person.

The exact form of the data and information which is retained on an individual's record will depend on the conditions to be satisfied for benefit entitlement. In an earnings-related scheme, it will be necessary to record periods and amounts of contributions, the registration number(s) of the employer(s) who paid them and, perhaps, the amount of earnings received in the relevant periods.

In a wage class scheme, similar information is necessary except that only the wage class of contribution paid will need to be identified.

In a flat-rate scheme, it will usually suffice to record the period and number of contributions paid and, where the insured population is divided into groups or classes which are covered for different contingencies, an indication of the class will also be needed.

Under the payroll systems of contribution payments, individual records should provide a historical record for each person in a form which provides direct and totally reliable evidence on which to determine benefit entitlement. It will be apparent that, under earnings-related and payroll schemes, the individual records are inevitably more detailed than under flat-rate schemes. It will be equally apparent that the transfer and recording of data, from contribution schedules provided by employers, is a complex operation which must be accurate and must *always* be kept up to date.

It is essential that this transfer of data to individual records is a continuous process, subjected to a rigid timetable, in order to prevent any build-up of arrears which would inevitably cause considerable administrative repercussions. Reference has already been made to the importance of reconciliation action, at the time of receipt of employer schedules, and a particular priority should be to reconcile any incorrectly coded names and/or social security numbers so that all contributions included on schedules can be brought to individual member accounts. Unallocated contributions are a major headache for many schemes and everything possible must be done to prevent the problem.

Many computerized systems have inbuilt programmes which prevent contributions remaining unallocated, for example by triggering registration action if an employee, who is shown on the schedule to have paid contributions, does not appear to have a social security number.

With social insurance schemes, the individual contribution record is generally only regarded as a record of insurable employment, not as an accounting document. It is not practical to make a comparison of the total amounts recorded on individual records with balances in the organization's accounts.

Once the work of transferring particulars — from an employer's contribution schedule to individual member records — has been completed and checked, the records become independent of the schedule. However, the total amounts due from the employer, as shown on the schedules, is an accounting item and schedules therefore become accounting documents used by the accounting department.

G. *Centralized and decentralized records*

The question of whether records should be held centrally or at the regional or local level of the organization will be determined by a number of factors, not least the type of scheme in operation, together with practical considerations such as the level of development of the country's infrastructure.

As has been seen, modern "on-line" EDP systems will often enable the organization to have a computerized data base which is accessible to all parts and at all levels of the organization. In this situation, it will clearly be suitable to retain records — particularly computerized contribution records — centrally.

Where manual systems are still operating, or where computerization has not yet reached the fully networked stage of development, other factors will affect decisions about the location of records. In countries where there is considerable movement of workers from one area to another; where communication facilities are inadequate; where there is a low density of scheme members in some areas, a centralized system of record keeping may be preferable.

On the other hand, in a country with large geographical regions/zones/provinces, with little movement of workers beyond those and with good communications networks, it may be more appropriate for records to be held at the regional or provincial level.

It should have become apparent from the preceding paragraphs that many factors will have an impact on the decision to centralize or decentralize records and that very careful consideration is needed before the decision is made.

What should be avoided, wherever possible, is the maintenance of sets of duplicated records, for example at the central *and* local levels. This arrangement obviously doubles the volume of records to be maintained and stored, increases demands on human and physical resources, and also increases the likelihood of erroneous records or contribution accounts.

H. Storage and destruction of records

The storage of the social security organization's records, whether they be contributions records or any other type, can give rise to major storage problems. There are no hard and fast rules for storage of records but some countries have statutes which require authorities and organizations to retain them for specific or minimum periods.

In general terms, it is essential to retain original records for as long as they are likely to affect the rights of the members protected by the scheme. With those systems which efficiently and safely transfer data and information from contribution schedules to individual records, it may be safe to destroy the schedules after a certain period of time. Where, however, the schedules are likely to be used as a source document at some future time, they may need to be retained indefinitely.

Some organizations use microfilm techniques to store records. This enables large quantities of data and information to be stored in a relatively small space. Clearly, however, where the microfilm is used as a duplicate or back-up copy, it *must* be stored in a different location to the original. Where it is the *only* record, security and safe-keeping are obviously even more vital.

Looking beyond the immediate question of retention of contribution records, it is appropriate to make a general reference to document storage and destruction. Most organizations operate a system of periodic weeding and destruction. The aim is, firstly, to keep readily at hand those documents and records which are likely to be referred to frequently; secondly, to "weed out" — or separate from the main storage — those documents which are expected to be required for reference only very infrequently; and finally, after an appropriate time lapse, to destroy those documents or records which are not going to be needed again.

A lead is usually taken from legal and/or auditing requirements, which will often specify the minimum retention period for certain types of document. As seen already, many documents and records will be needed throughout the *insurance* lifetime of the scheme member — indeed often the *actual* life time and beyond. Other documents and records will, on the other hand, have a limited use or value.

There may also be a need for modifications of weeding and destruction systems, for example, where certain documents may be removed from main or master files, then set aside for a specific period at the end of which (if not required or used in the meantime) they are destroyed. It is rarely possible to destroy *any* documents or records immediately after use and it will generally be necessary to retain most items for at least three years.

The important point to remember, as with all other aspects of social security administration, is that careful research and consideration is needed *before* procedures are adopted. This is especially the case when making decisions about storage, retention and destruction of documents and records.

ADMINISTRATION OF SOCIAL SECURITY

MODULE 4:
COMPLIANCE AND ENFORCEMENT

International Labour Office Geneva

MODULE CONTENTS

UNIT 1: **Compliance**

    A. The nature of compliance

    B. General approach to compliance

    C. Organization of compliance operations

    D. Powers of inspectors and inspection

UNIT 2: **Enforcement**

    A. Legislative aspects

    B. Recovery action, penalties and fines

    C. Prosecution

    D. The social security institution's Legal Division

MODULE 4

COMPLIANCE AND ENFORCEMENT

UNIT 1: Compliance

Introduction

The achievement and maintenance of satisfactory standards of compliance, with the legislation relating to payment of contributions, poses serious administrative problems for most social security organizations.

Compliance problems, whilst varying in complexity and intensity, are very common and social security schemes *must* take measures to ensure that contributions *are* collected. Those measures should include, where necessary, the prosecution of employers — to promote compliance with the law.

Compliance procedures are of basic importance in any contributory scheme and all social security schemes are engaged in a constant search for the most effective compliance procedures for their national social and economic conditions. Without a satisfactory level of compliance, a social security scheme cannot function and properly meet the needs of its members. One of the measures of success of a social security scheme is the extent of the acceptance of — and compliance with — the legislation.

A. The nature of compliance

An earlier unit pointed out that social security legislation will normally specify which establishments and employees are liable for payment of contributions, and that they are also required to register with the scheme. However, the registration of an establishment does not guarantee subsequent compliance with the scheme and there are always employers — and indeed scheme members — who will seek to evade their liabilities.

There are many forms of evasion. Some employers will claim to have fewer staff than the minimum figure for compulsory affiliation to the scheme. Others may under-report the number of employees or understate employee earnings on contribution schedules. Yet others are guilty of deducting the contribution from employees' pay but not remitting payment to the social security organization. These are only a few of the many types of non-compliance.

Defaulting employers often go to great lengths to avoid compliance, sometimes in collusion with the employees concerned. This clearly makes compliance action even more difficult.

Establishments which are in financial difficulties may go bankrupt or close down without warning. Some of them may then reopen, under a different name, in an attempt to avoid responsibility for arrears of contributions.

It may be surprising to learn that many employers, in attempting to evade compliance, will place difficulties and barriers in the way of any social security inspector trying to check on cases of non-compliance.

The range of problems encountered in implementing the legislation requires that a broad and imaginative approach be adopted if satisfactory levels of compliance are to be achieved. Such an approach might include, for example, well planned registration systems and effective contribution collection systems which quickly identify employers who do not comply on time. (One example is the survey card system which was referred to earlier).

B. General approach to compliance

When considering the organization of compliance work, it is necessary to take into account the attitudes of employers and employees to the scheme. If the scheme is well understood, is popular and has favourable publicity, then there will be a tendency towards a better general standard of cooperation with the social security administration. It therefore helps to have a well publicized scheme, because employers who have a real interest in the scheme, in their membership of the scheme, and in their employees in general, may be much more ready to cooperate with the administration. The value and importance of public relations will be examined in a later module.

Often, employers not only have to contribute relatively large amounts of money to the scheme but also have to cope with administrative tasks on behalf of the social security administration, which can be quite onerous. The majority of employers meet their obligations conscientiously but it is unrealistic to expect anything more than mere compliance with the rules and regulations.

In almost all schemes, there will be a proportion of employers who have a negative attitude towards the scheme, who are unwilling participants and who are always ready to take advantage of any loopholes in, or opportunities to evade, the law. These employers are to be found, mainly but not exclusively, amongst smaller businesses with limited resources and records. In the case of employers who keep inadequate records, the problem sometimes stems from a lack of knowledge, of understanding of the law, or of administrative capacity to comply with the law. For these reasons, it is always useful to produce, for issue to employers, a publication or guide which sets out employers' obligations in relation to the scheme.

As will be seen more fully in a later module, many social security administrations go to considerable lengths to inform and educate employers. A variety of methods are available, including: producing an employer's guide in different language versions; giving training sessions on social security administrative operations to representatives of businesses registered with the scheme (for example, personnel officers, wages clerks); giving talks to employers' or employees' associations, etc. These and other activities generally result in better standards of administration — and compliance — by employers.

An arrangement which can also be useful for the larger employers is the appointment, by them, of a liaison officer who then becomes the focal point for *all* social security matters. This can be of considerable use to both the employer and the social security administration. Not only does it facilitate contact on routine items but it also means that the employer's liaison officer has to accept responsibility for contribution returns, which also tends to encourage a personal interest in the accuracy of the information on schedules and payment remittances.

It is important that the social security administration's own staff — especially inspectorate staff and those dealing most directly with employers and contributions issues — attempt to understand the viewpoint of employers and the implications for compliance operations. There are many practical steps which can be used to promote full cooperation with the administration. Time spent in developing good working relationships with employers must never be regarded as time wasted; it is almost always time well spent. Such an approach is usually far better than a coercive one, which should only be necessary in a minority of cases. Employers clearly vary considerably in their attitudes and capacities and therefore need to be treated differently and individually.

A final observation on the general approach to compliance work is that speedy attention to compliance problems is always necessary, in order to ensure that problems are not worsened further because of delays in addressing them.

C. Organization of compliance operations

The inspectorate has a critical role in compliance work and it is essential that the inspectorate's workload is well organized. An aid to successful compliance work is sound and comprehensive legislation, which minimizes questions and doubts about liability, classification, due dates for remittances, etc., and which also makes clear the penalties for failure to comply with the legislation.

The most successful arrangement is for inspectors to operate at the local level and to be under the operational control of, and attached to, the contributions section. In smaller offices, an inspector may also be in charge of the contributions section or perhaps attached to a larger office in the vicinity. Inspectors have a vital function as people who are charged with the initial enforcement of the law which, together with the inspections of establishments, is their main duty. However, as the main contact point between the scheme and employers, the inspector is effectively the representative of the scheme which inevitably extends his responsibilities beyond compliance, into public relations and educational activities.

Inspectors must be carefully selected and well trained. A balance then has to be struck between leaving them long enough, on a tour of duty, to become experienced and effective but not so long as to increase the risk of complicity with employers. Many social security administrations therefore restrict the period of time spent on inspectorate work to ensure that the law is enforced impartially. Social security organizations which, for whatever reasons, need to retain the same inspectors for several years may find it adviseable to move them, periodically, to a new area.

Large social security organizations which have many inspectors, will also probably have senior inspectors, either at local or regional level, who supervise, monitor and control the work of the inspectorate team. Senior inspectors would also deal with especially difficult inspections or important cases (for example those involving prosecution), give advice and guidance, and assist with the training and development of inspectors working for them.

The organization of the inspectorate's workload should be complemented by the thorough planning of its execution. The two main aspects are setting targets and control of inspectors' activities. Some would argue that the variable nature of inspections, and the difficulty of effectively supervising the work undertaken away from the office, means that little can be done in respect of targets and, particularly, control. These clearly *are* limiting factors but it should be remembered that workloads *have* to be quantified in order to determine staffing requirements. Senior or experienced inspectors are in a position to do this and to evaluate reports of work completed and cleared. It is therefore perfectly feasible to set specific targets, taking into account the number, size, nature and location of establishments.

One factor which affects targets, output, clearance rates, etc., is transportation arrangements. It goes without saying that fewer visits are likely to be made if inspectors are "on foot" or are totally dependent on public transport than if they use private or official vehicles. Assignments need to be properly planned, not only by way of dealing with more or less urgent cases in priority order but also in the routing of visits, choosing times of day most suitable to particular employers, trying to plan for a series of visits in adjacent areas or districts, etc.

Close monitoring by senior inspectors, often using daily inspectorate activity reports, will usually reveal badly organized and inefficient practices. It is therefore essential that activities *are* closely monitored and supervised and that inspectors — especially those who are new and inexperienced — are not permitted to develop bad habits or inefficient methods.

Views differ as to whether inspections should be carried out with or without prior notice. In the case of establishments with a satisfactory compliance record, it is often advantageous to pre-notify the employer. This enables the assembly of records, documents, etc., before the inspector arrives and is likely to save time and facilitate the task. This is preferable to the loss of time which occurs when inspectors are unable to carry out un-notified, "surprise" inspections or when such inspections take an inordinate length of time.

Nevertheless, this does not rule out the occasional unannounced visit, as a matter of policy. Although uncooperative establishments may react badly to surprise inspections, these are likely to be more productive — unless the inspector is obstructed. The alternative choice, pre-arranged inspections, whilst not necessarily leading to fuller cooperation, may risk concealment of the records (and, in some situations, even the personnel) needed to ascertain true liability. It is, however, occasionally useful to use surprise follow-up visits for assessing the extent to which establishments have improved their compliance activities following earlier inspectorate action.

The emphasis which has been placed in this manual on the organization of compliance work underlines the fact that it is of critical importance to all social security administrations.

D. Powers of inspectors and inspection

Social security legislation should provide for the appointment of inspectors and set out the rules governing their right of entry into registered establishments. The legislation should normally also confer upon them investigative powers, including the examination of pertinent documents. Their main function is to enforce liability of covered establishments by ensuring that those who come within the scope of the law are duly registered, and that registered establishments comply fully and correctly with the contribution regulations. This entails periodic checks of pay and personnel records, interviews with employees and scrutiny of the copies of returns and schedules submitted with remittances.

Inspections and other visits have to be carried out with tact, firmness and impartiality. Establishments which are well-organized and cooperative will pose few problems. However, inspectors often have serious difficulties gaining entry to premises, or access to records, where the employer is in arrears or is unwilling to meet his obligations to submit evidential returns, schedules, etc., at the prescribed intervals. Sometimes the most difficult establishments to deal with are large government departments, state or parastatal organizations, which may have inadequate records of the workers covered by the scheme. These organizations are often less susceptible to pressure to comply with the law.

Fig. 14:

"... inspections have to be carried out with tact, firmness ... (but)
... inspectors need adequate powers"

Inspectors need adequate powers and legal remedies to counteract obstruction in the discharge of their duties. It is often possible to use devices such as social security clearance certificates as an instrument of persuasion for employers to pay arrears of contributions. It is also essential that they have support, from senior inspectors and from the administration as a whole, if they are to succeed in enforcing the law.

It is usual to require inspectors to provide a written report following each visit, in a standard format, detailing the action, findings, and — if appropriate — recommendations for further action. In addition to inspections, the outstanding queries and problems arising from the processing of contribution returns and schedules will also be passed to inspectors for action and resolution.

Control and direction of the inspectorate is necessary if the optimum use is to be made of what are often limited manpower resources. It is wise to lay down a policy for inspections and other inspectorate tasks so that those resources are deployed in the most effective way. Efforts should be made to ensure that the work of the collective inspectorate, and of individual inspectors, is efficiently organized.

Some social security organizations are without an inspection policy; others have one only in vague or general terms. Many have found, from experience, that it is desirable to stipulate a specific number of inspections, of each registered establishment, over a particular period. Another approach is to regulate the frequency of inspections per establishment, in accordance with their compliance records. Thus, delinquent employers would be visited more frequently than the reliable ones.

It is common to find tasks being given to inspectors which divert them away from their main duty — enforcement, primarily through inspections. Many routine contribution queries can be resolved through correspondence or telephone/fax communications. Many which do require contact with the employer can be cleared by arranging for the employer's liaison officer, or another representative of the employer, to visit the local office. An alternative is to send a reliable member of the local office staff, other than the inspector, to the employer's premises — usually by appointment — to collect the information. These are some of the ways in which work activities can be organized so as to divert the more straightforward cases to other staff, thus providing more time for the inspector to deal with complex and serious cases.

Benefit claims may also give rise to problems which are passed to inspectors but the same rules should be applied, i.e. only those with serious features should be dealt with by inspectors.

UNIT 2: Enforcement

A. Legislative aspects

An earlier unit pointed out that most social security legislation provides for the levying of fines in respect of late paid contributions. Many schemes also include legal recovery procedures, through distraint. This is a process whereby anyone has the right to seize and sell a debtor's goods or property in order to obtain the monies owing. Civil and criminal actions are also usually available to the social security administration for pursuance of a debt.

Where non-compliance is of a very serious nature, independent recovery machinery of the type referred to above is very necessary. Usually, it is only as a last resort that such extreme measures are taken because there is always the chance that they may result in the closure or bankruptcy of an enterprise or company — with a consequent loss of jobs for the employees involved (i.e. social security members).

A real dilemma may exist where the law is persistently flouted and the financial position of the enterprise is so weak that it is unable to pay both the current contributions and the outstanding arrears.

Social security legislation should include a list of offences, for example, fraudulent claims to benefit, the making of false statements, failure to pay social security contributions, failure to pay contributions on time, etc., for which prosecution may be brought.

As mentioned previously, there is an understandable reluctance, on the part of some social security institutions, to prosecute offenders for contribution arrears for fear that the enterprise may have to close down. However, provided that the penalties contained in the legislation are reasonable and appropriate — yet at the same time meaningful the Institution should normally be able to count on public support for prosecutions. The social security institution can expect to be seen, by the scheme's participants as a whole, as fulfilling its duty to them by prosecuting offenders.

In some instances, criminal prosecutions for serious offences are additionally justified for their deterrent effect on potential offenders. Failure to prosecute cases which involve blatant breaches of the law, or to secure appropriate penalties, may bring the scheme into disrepute. Such failure may also encourage the belief that the legislation can be infringed without regard to, or fear of, the consequences.

However, although it is difficult to see how the more persistent offenders can be dealt with unless severe sanctions *are* imposed, these questions have to be decided on a case-by-case basis. If, for any reason, legal action is generally ruled out, it is absolutely essential that the other forms of compliance action, used by the social security institution, are very well organized and effective — so as to ensure that standards of compliance *are* satisfactory.

Some social security institutions argue that public education is more appropriate and effective than legislative action, especially in newly implemented schemes. This rarely proves to be the case. What is needed is an effective combination of information and publicity, education, and the threat of legal action. But it is also important that legal action is not seen only as a possibility but rather as a certainty for those who flout the law.

With public education in mind, it is important that all appropriate publicity material — leaflets, forms, demands for arrears, etc., — should include a reference to the consequences of failing to comply with the legal requirements of the scheme.

B. Recovery action, penalties and fines

Procedures for recovery of contribution arrears range from cases dealt with in their entirety by correspondence to those which end up in the courts. In most cases, the speedier the action to determine and enforce liability, the easier it is to settle the case. However, it is always necessary to be prepared for those which entail legal action.

An earlier unit pointed out that it is usual for social security legislation to require that contributions be paid by a due date — usually within a given number of days after a calendar month-end. It is also common for legislation to contain provisions for the levying of surcharges — usually by way of interest and/or fines — in respect of any contributions which are "late paid", i.e. paid after the due date.

Surcharges should be designed to deter enterprises from persistent late payment and therefore need to be at a reasonable percentage of the amount of the overdue payment. Many schemes have a surcharge which is progressively increased in relation to the length of time by which payment is delayed.

Nevertheless, it is important not to set surcharges too low or the enterprise will find it advantageous to withhold payment and utilize the funds for business purposes. Furthermore, the administrative cost of recovery may be greater than the surcharge.

It was also mentioned previously that social security schemes can institute court action to recover debts — e.g. overdue contributions. The legal recovery procedures are usually modelled on procedures for the recovery of unpaid taxes. Bearing in mind the potential problems of legal action — including the risk of closure of the enterprise — recovery is often effected by making arrangements for payment by instalments. These should be set at a level which is reasonable, both from the point of view of the employer *and* of the social security institution.

In those cases where bankruptcy does occur, the legislation should provide for priority to be given to the social security debts — in the interests of the workers who paid contributions which were then retained by the employer and are due to the scheme. It is often the case that a country's legislation gives the social security institution the second claim on the enterprise's assets — after the tax authority's claim.

C. Prosecution

Reference has already been made to the part which legal action may need to play in the recovery of arrears of contributions, and to other offences which may result in the prosecution of an employer (or indeed a member) for example for false statements, fraudulent claims, etc.

Whatever the reason for the prosecution, it is essential that the institution takes very seriously the approach to prosecution procedures.

The design and implementation of those procedures must be such that, in each case where it is decided to prosecute, there is a very high likelihood of success. It was seen earlier that a valuable bi-product of the successful prosecution of offenders is the deterrent effect on other potential offenders. If the institution develops a reputation for unsuccessful prosecutions — whether because of weak cases or poorly presented prosecution — that deterrent value will be negated. For these reasons, many social security institutions tend to be very selective in the cases which they decide to prosecute.

Experience shows that, where a prosecution fails, it is often because a case has been badly or carelessly prepared. It is essential, therefore, not only that procedures are well designed but that they are meticulously followed. Rules of evidence must be carefully obeyed, supporting evidence and related documentation must be without fault and no risks should be taken in the preparation or presentation of a case.

It cannot be over-emphasized how important it is to achieve and maintain a consistently high degree of success in the institution's prosecution activity.

D. The social security institution's Legal Division

Given the importance of the social security legislation to the successful operation of the scheme, it is inevitable that a social security organization must include a Legal Division. The Division may be large or small, depending on the size of the institution and its range of social security activities. It may have one or more legally qualified personnel in addition to support staff; it may be centrally located (usually as part of the headquarters unit) or regionally based. Whatever its organizational position, the Legal Division will normally have responsibilities beyond those relating to compliance. It will not only serve the need for prosecution of offenders — referred to in the earlier paragraphs relating to non-compliance — but also for clarification and interpretation of the legislation, for drafting additional or amending legislation, and perhaps also for keeping abreast of other (non-social security) legislation which might impact on the institution.

In this section of the manual, however, the focus is on compliance and enforcement. In this context, the importance of the Legal Division is usually related to the preparation of the documents supporting the prosecution, or the examination, checking and correction of those documents if prepared elsewhere in the organization.

The actual prosecution of the case in court may be made by a member of the Legal Division's staff but, in some institutions, it will be undertaken by a senior — and very experienced — inspector, or perhaps someone from the regional/headquarters compliance division. In very complex cases it is sometimes necessary for the social security institution to engage the services of a barrister but, in the majority of prosecutions, it is usual for in-house personnel to present the case.

Although the reference to prosecution procedures, the need for a Legal Division, and its role and responsibilities, is included in this Module dealing with compliance activities, it should be remembered that compliance will form only a part of the Legal Division's workload and that it is just as likely to be involved in other administrative areas, including benefit operations.

ADMINISTRATION OF SOCIAL SECURITY

MODULE 5:
AWARD AND PAYMENT OF BENEFITS

International Labour Office Geneva

MODULE CONTENTS

UNIT 1:   **Benefit awards**

    A.   An overview of the range of benefits

    B.   Key elements of benefit procedures

    C.   Satisfying the qualifying conditions

    D.   Procedures for the award of benefit

    E.   Adjudication procedures

    F.   Notifying decisions to members

UNIT 2:   **Payment of benefit**

    A.   Methods of payment

    B.   Organizational considerations

    C.   Payment authorization

    D.   Security requirements

    E.   Audit and survey functions

UNIT 3:   **Appeals procedures**

    A.   Rights of appeal and the appeals system

    B.   The constitution of appeal tribunals

    C.   Appeals procedure

    D.   Decisions and reviews

MODULE 5

AWARD AND PAYMENT OF BENEFITS

Introduction

This module will examine the "end-product" of the social security scheme, what social security provides by way of benefits for individuals and families for whom this is perhaps the most important aspect of a scheme. Attention will focus on the material benefits, the conditions to be satisfied for entitlement, and the procedures to be followed for the award and payment — or refusal — of benefits.

A former Director-General of the ILO, Wilfred Jenks, said in an address in 1971:

"Nothing in the history of social policy has transformed the life of the common man ... more ... than the assurance that, in the event of loss of income through accident, poor health, unemployment, death .... he will not be forced into destitution".

Social insurance has long been thought of as the first pillar of security, through income replacement, when earnings were interrupted or stopped altogether. A second pillar soon followed — the provision of medical care for insured persons and, often, for their families. A third pillar has also been added in many countries — represented by a variety of programmes of financial assistance which support those people whose means and resources are meagre, whose family responsibilities make a special claim on the community, or who have special needs or circumstances which warrant extra help.

This manual, however, deals primarily with only the first of those three pillars — social insurance. Manual number 5 of this series deals with social health insurance (the second pillar) and, although there is no specific reference in this administration manual to (what is widely referred to as) social assistance (the third pillar), much of the content applies equally to the administration of social assistance as to social insurance. The main difference between the two is the basis of entitlement — contributory in the case of social insurance, non-contributory in the case of social assistance.

UNIT 1: Benefit awards

A. An overview of the range of benefits

The range and variety of benefits provided by social security schemes throughout the world clearly varies enormously. The most highly developed schemes embrace a comprehensive range, whilst the least developed may offer only the most basic cover.

Benefits are grouped, under ILO Convention No. 102 (1952), in a way which has regard to their functions and which only imposes minimum conditions that all countries — industrialized and developing — can build upon at the appropriate time, as their schemes continue to develop.

The benefits included in the Convention are:

- medical care
- sickness benefit
- maternity benefit
- unemployment benefit
- family benefit
- employment injury benefit
- invalidity benefit
- old-age benefit
- survivors' benefit

As varied as the range of benefits which are included in schemes, is the way in which their administration is organized. Having regard to the list above, however, there are some broad similarities of approach.

Health care is generally administered by an institution other than the social security organization. Unemployment benefit is often administered in tandem with an employment service, for example by a department within the Ministry of Labour. The remaining seven contingencies are normally the responsibility of the social security institution.

It is also common practice for institutions to separate the administration of benefits into "short-term" and "long-term" benefit divisions; this is not only for administrative convenience but also because it enables greater specialization and thus — in theory at least — greater expertise and efficiency.

It is therefore quite common practice to organize the processing of benefit claims in that way, with one group of staff dealing with old-age and survivors' benefits (long-term benefits) and another group dealing with sickness and maternity (short-term) benefits. Invalidity benefit, which often follows on when sickness benefit entitlement is exhausted, is also often dealt with by the short-term benefits group.

Where an employment injury benefit scheme operates alongside — and is administered together with — the social insurance scheme, it is quite common to find claims to employment injury benefit being processed by the short-term benefit group, as there is usually a limitation on the period of payment. Any resulting long-term disablement benefit (e.g. a disability pension) which succeeds the injury benefit period will generally be dealt with by the long-term benefit group.

B. Key elements of benefit procedures

When considering the procedures for processing claims to any cash benefit, it is important to remember the primary aim of social security benefits: to replace — wholly or partially — the resulting loss of earnings following the interruption or cessation of employment.

That aim is *not* met if the member has to wait several weeks or months before receiving benefit. One of the main challenges, for any social security institution, must therefore be to ensure that benefit procedures are designed to achieve one of the institution's key objectives — paying benefit promptly and accurately.

It therefore follows that systems and procedures for making and processing claims, determining entitlement, and for calculating and paying benefits, must be as simple and straightforward as possible, and easily understood by members. At the same time, however, those procedures must also be designed in such a way as to prevent or detect fraudulent claims, or abuse of the scheme.

The key elements of benefit procedures, and of processing claims to benefits, embrace a number of features. There are conditions which need to be satisfied (to be dealt with in the next section) along with straightforward but secure methods for making and receiving claims, accompanied by effective and efficient procedures for establishing title, calculating, and paying the benefit. These elements apply to all schemes, regardless of whether the procedures are entirely manual or where calculation and payment procedures are highly computerized.

Very often the legislation also sets limits to the maximun duration of benefits and this places a demand on the institution's procedures, which must ensure that payment o benefit does not extend beyond that period.

It is clear, therefore, when benefit procedures are being designed, developed, modified or improved, that mechanisms must be put in place which will ensure that:

- the procedures for making claims are kept as simple as possible — commensurate with adequate safeguards against fraud and abuse;

- benefit claims are processed quickly, efficiently and accurately, with an absolute minimum of bureaucracy;

- decisions on entitlement — or refusals, where appropriate — are made speedily;

- payment is made promptly, when due;

- that the staff of the institution who are responsible for processing claims are well trained, knowledgeable, efficient — and also conscious of the importance of the benefit payments to the individual member.

Fig. 15:
"... when benefit procedures are being designed ..."

SOCIAL SECURITY INSTITUTION
BENEFIT PROCEDURES SECTION

BENEFITS

DESIGN CHECK LIST
☑ SIMPLE PROCEDURE
☑ SAFE
☑ QUICK
☑ EFFICIENT
☑ PROMPT PAYMENT
☑ WELL TRAINED STAFF
☑ ETC
☑ ETC

C. Satisfying the qualifying conditions

All schemes require that certain conditions are to be met before benefits can be awarded. A basic condition is that the claimant is properly within the coverage of the scheme. There are various other conditions which have to be satisfied which depend on the type of benefit being claimed and the contingency it is designed to meet. *Proof* of the contingency for which the scheme — or the particular benefit — was designed is also a key condition. For example, when sickness benefit is claimed, evidence must be produced to confirm that there *is* a medical condition which is causing incapacity for work; when employment injury benefit is claimed, it must be shown that the incapacity *is* the result of a work-related injury/occupational disease; those claiming an old-age pension must show that they *have* reached the age stipulated by the regulations, and so on.

In many cases, an award of benefit is also dependent upon the actual reduction or cessation of earnings, upon the need to incur certain expenses, or on confirmation of a particular condition, e.g. pregnancy, death, the presence of dependants, etc. It is therefore necessary for the social security institution to be satisfied that *all relevant* conditions are fulfilled.

However, it may not always be necessary to test *all* the conditions. For example, if the rules require that, in order to qualify for benefit, an individual must have been insured at a given point in time but it is found that this condition is not satisfied — then there is clearly no point in going on to test other conditions.

Even when the basic conditions *are* satisfied, there may be additional qualifying conditions. Take for example a requirement which is common to many insurance schemes — that a minimum period must be served (often varying in length with the type of benefit) before title can succeed. Such a test is usually necessary in order to reduce the possibility that persons will seek to enter covered (insured) employment because they know that an event has occurred, or is imminent, which gives rise to benefit.

It should also be mentioned in passing that, in social assistance (or general revenue financed) schemes, since the claimant is not personally insured under the scheme and cannot therefore be identified from insurance records, some other method of determining eligibility must be used. In most cases, a simple test of nationality or residency is all that is required; means are usually also assessed. Proof of residence is required, this being greater for the longer-term (old-age or invalidity) benefits than for benefits of shorter duration.

Once proof of the contingency has been provided, and all the other relevant conditions are shown to be satisfied, then — and only then — can the type and amount of the appropriate benefit be established and payment made.

Finally, in this section dealing with qualifying conditions, reference must be made to one particular administrative aspect related to the application of contribution conditions. Where it is necessary to establish the details of a claimant's individual contribution record, before title to benefit can be decided, it is essential that the record can be retrieved quickly. It therefore follows, regardless of whether the institution is using manual or computerized systems, that the procedures do provide for ready access to such records. Moreover, this requirement also demands that individual contribution records are kept absolutely up to date. If the processing of a benefit claim is delayed by the need for lengthy enquiries to establish the claimant's contribution record, prompt payment will not be achieved.

It also follows that one of the key elements of benefit procedures is a prompt and efficient system for recording contribution payments (referred to earlier in the manual).

D. Procedures for the award of benefit

In a well-conceived and well-designed social security organization, the teamwork of the whole system is ultimately focused upon the benefits staff, particularly those at the local/regional level who are responsible for processing claims.

Ideally, legislation will have been drafted in such a way as to enable the qualifying conditions to be satisfied and verified without time-wasting correspondence. In order to achieve this, it is important to bring together executive staff and policy/legal experts at an early stage of the planning process.

Finance procedures should also be designed so that the local/regional office always has a ready means of immediate payment for its regular claims load and also for emergencies.

One type of emergency, which will periodically effect social security offices, is an epidemic. It is usual practice for social security institutions to prepare plans in anticipation — "emergency plans". This invariably means ensuring that the in-office training programme enables the suspension of most other office operations, in order that the maximum number of staff — pre-trained against such an eventuality — can be diverted from their normal duties to assist with the processing of benefit claims.

When considering benefit award procedures, it is important to remember that recipients of cash benefits — the beneficiaries — are also entitled to know *how* the benefit calculation was made. They should not be left to wonder if — or assume that — the payment *is* correct. The award procedure should therefore include a written notification for the beneficiary giving details of the benefit award. This usually involves the issue of a simple printed notification setting out — as a minimum — the period for which benefit is payable, the weekly rate payable and any special conditions which apply to the receipt or payment of the benefit. It is also usual to include, amongst the information on such notifications, some reference to the beneficiary's appeal rights. (Unit 3 of this module will examine appeals procedures.)

E. Adjudication procedures

A potential beneficiary, having submitted a claim to benefit, should be able to expect to be informed whether or not the claim has succeeded. Before that can be done, however, someone in the social security institution has first to *decide* whether or not the claim has succeeded. Social security legislation therefore usually confers, on certain members of the institution's staff, the authority to give decisions on benefit claims. Traditionally, the more complex the claim, or the more long-term the potential award, the more senior is the official who will decide. Social security regulations usually provide such authority for the institution's personnel and often also include a provision for the appointment of adjudication officers and adjudication procedures.

In theory this means that each time a member of the staff of the institution decides to pay (or refuse) benefit, this represents a formal decision which will carry certain rights of appeal for the claimant (as a later section in this module will show).

In practice, particularly in routinely straightforward cases, the fact of processing a successful claim and making a payment of benefit implies the entitlement. Generally, it is only claims that are refused (disallowed) which warrant the direct involvement of an adjudication officer, or perhaps those paid at less than the standard rate.

Whatever the legislation or system, it is essential that there are regulated and formal rules and procedures for deciding favourably or unfavourably on *each* individual claim to benefit.

The social security institution's in-house procedural instructions must always make clear which level or grade of officer can give a decision on which type of case. It must be clear to all staff which cases fall within their own level of competence to decide, and which cases they must refer to a more senior colleague, supervisor, manager, or to a specially authorized (and appropriately trained) adjudication officer.

Regardless of the specific procedures adopted, it is essential that *all* decisions are given in writing, and thus permanently recorded.

F. *Notifying decisions to members*

Brief reference was made, in the section dealing with benefit award procedures (Section D above), to the need for explanations to be given to beneficiaries showing how benefit entitlement had been calculated.

Everyone who makes a claim for benefit should be able to expect to receive a written notification of the result of that claim and this applies whether the claim is successful or not. Where successful, the notification will often be a simple form, advising the member of the period for which benefit is awarded and the weekly rate payable. Some claims are unsuccessful, however, for example because the conditions for receipt of benefit are not satisfied, and are therefore rejected (disallowed). Others are only partially payable, for example because insufficient contributions have been paid to qualify for the full rate of benefit. Yet others cannot be processed because information or evidence is missing from the claim. Whatever the result of the claim, it is important that the member is notified — in writing.

Some institutions are guilty of simply letting unsuccessful or unresolved claims "rest" in pending trays, taking no action to notify members of the results of a claim and — even more seriously — failing to notify them of their appeal rights.

Most social security organizations therefore produce a series of pre-printed letters or notifications — "forms" — which are used to inform members of the result of their claims. A small series of individually tailored forms will cover the majority of types of benefit claims, decisions and situations. The less common and more complex cases usually warrant an individually prepared notification (perhaps an individual letter) for the member, which fully explains the decision given on the particular claim.

Thus, each member should be able to expect an individual, personal notification of the result of each claim which they make. It is important that the social security institution regards the issue of such notifications as an integral part of the benefit decision — making process; it should *not* be regarded as an additional task or burden for the institution's staff, created by the scheme members.

UNIT 2: Payment of benefit

A. Methods of payment

As with many other aspects of social security organization, the methods used for the payment of benefits will be heavily influenced by the level of development of the country's infrastructure. Countries in which the banking system is well developed, where telecommunication installations are advanced, and which have nationwide postal services, will have a greater choice of payment methods than countries lacking such facilities.

The most basic schemes will perhaps depend almost entirely on some form of cash payment to the member, sometimes made through a system of locally based paying agents. The more advanced systems are able to make direct payments of benefit into individual members' bank accounts, by regular direct transfer. In between those two ends of the spectrum will be found a variety of payment systems, closely tailored to the needs of both the institution and its members but also, as already indicated, heavily influenced by infrastructural factors.

Where the country has a network of local post offices, it is common to make benefit payments by (a type of) cheque. Where the country's postal service is also sufficiently well developed so as to enable mail to be delivered to members' homes (or to private post office boxes) then the payment cheques will normally be sent by post.

For long-term benefits, particularly pensions of one type or another, many countries make regular payments by order book which consist of a series of detachable orders and permanent counterfoils. The order book is presented by the claimant, weekly or monthly as the case may be, at the local post office for payment. As each order is encashed, the post office removes and retains the order, which is eventually returned to the social security organization for reconciliation action, leaving the related counterfoil in the order book as evidence of payment.

The most advanced institutions are able to prepare, produce, and issue cheques and order books by computer, but many organizations still have to depend on manually produced instruments of payment. Wherever possible, payment methods should be developed which do *not* involve the handling of cash by the institution's staff. The aim should be, so far as is possible, to utilize existing postal or banking facilities and to enable members to collect cash payments with as little inconvenience as possible. It is also important to strike reasonable balance between convenience for the member and for the social security institution. Additionally, it is necessary to have due regard to the administrative costs, for the organization will almost certainly be required to pay for any services provided by post offices, banks, agents, and the like.

Where alternative facilities *do* exist, payment by cash, directly to the member, is usually reserved for cases where any other method would involve unacceptable risks of loss of other types of instruments of payment.

Fig. 16:
"... choice of payment methods ..."

When payment methods are being designed or developed it is important to have regard to *all* the factors mentioned already but also to security aspects, which are dealt with in Unit 2D.

Finally, in this section dealing with payment methods, it should not be forgotten that a number of social security schemes now rely heavily on employers to pay benefits (primarily short-term benefits) on behalf of the organization, at least for the first few weeks or months of interruption of work. This development has been prompted by the fact that, increasingly, employers are "topping up" benefits by paying all or part of the shortfall between the benefit level and the normal wage/salary.

Administratively, it makes sense for the employer to pay both elements together (benefit *plus* any wage/salary due) rather than have both the employer *and* the social security institution making parallel payments. The employer is then subsequently reimbursed or, more commonly, recovers the payment of benefit, made on behalf of the institution, from the next contribution remittance.

This is also usually far more convenient for members, as the total income during their illness comes from the one source — the "normal source" — the employer.

This type of arrangement generally lasts for only a limited period (usually not more than six months) after which time the social security institution assumes responsibility for (longer-term) benefit payments.

Clearly, such procedures have to be laid down in legislation, and rights and obligations for all parties must be made clear therein.

B. Organizational considerations

All the procedural stages of processing and paying benefits are underscored by the need to balance speed and efficiency on the one hand with tight security and control of public monies on the other. Bearing in mind, yet again, how important it is to members that benefits are paid promptly, it is nevertheless vital that adequate care is taken by the institution to safeguard public funds from abuse.

This balance is not easy to achieve. It is possible to design procedures which make it extremely difficult for members to obtain benefits to which they are not entitled; checks and counterchecks can be built into processing procedures to reduce the risk of wrong payments. However, the consequence is protracted procedures, delays in payments to members and higher administrative costs. The converse is fewer checks, quicker processing times, speedier payments — but a greater risk of wrong payment and a higher incidence of procedural errors. The solution is often to design procedures in such a way that the vast majority of cases, which are "straightforward" and which have a relatively low risk factor, can be dealt with routinely, quickly and with a minimum of checks; whilst the "unusual", more complex cases will attract a greater level of scrutiny. This approach often involves selective use of pre- and post-payment checks; pre-payment checks being made on high risk cases and post-payment checks for low risk — i.e. the majority — of claims.

Another important organizational consideration is that of segregating claims processing and calculation of benefit entitlement from the payment process. It is essential to ensure that different staff are employed on the preparation and issue of payments to those who were responsible for the calculation. The more staff that are involved in the overall process, the harder it is for collusion to take place between them and, thus, the lower is the risk of internal fraud. At the same time, however, the "balance" referred to previously requires that not so many staff are involved so as to lead to long processing times, with consequent delays in payments to members.

C. *Payment authorization*

With both organizational considerations *and* security requirements in mind, payment of benefit is an activity which must be approved or agreed by an official of the social security institution who is authorized to give that approval.

The legislation and/or regulations will normally specify which group/level/grade of officer is empowered to authorize payments. A payment of benefit can then *only* be made if such an officer has authorized that payment. This mechanism is usually the primary check, designed to prevent payments being made to anyone other than a legitimate beneficiary.

In addition to the security consideration, however, the authorization procedure embodies another important element of benefit awards — that of the need for a formal award by an authorized official of the institution. Such officers are often referred to as "independent statutory authorities", authorized under the legislation (statutes) to give decisions on claims — in this example, the decision is to pay benefit.

It is important that the procedures for authorizing payments of benefits make it impossible for the same person to calculate entitlement *and* authorize a payment. This division and segregation of responsibility is essential in order to reduce the possibility of internal fraud or abuse, and to remove the possibility of a member of the institution's staff processing a spurious claim in their personal favour. As already pointed out, the more personnel who are involved in the payment process, the more difficult it becomes to commit internal fraud; firstly because there are more people who need to be complicit before the fraud can be committed and, secondly, because the more who are involved, the more likely it is that the fraud will be discovered.

Fig. 17:
*"... division of responsibility
... reduces the risk of internal
fraud"*

D. Security requirements

The previous section touched upon one of the basic security requirements — that of segregating benefit calculation from award and payment authorization. However, there are many other requirements which are necessary in order to safeguard public monies.

Whichever types of instruments of payment are used — benefit cheques, order books, direct transfer to members' bank accounts, etc. — it is essential that, at each stage of the payment process, any member of staff who has had a part to play in that process can subsequently be identified.

With manual systems this invariably requires the signature of each individual at each stage of the process, for example signing to acknowledge receipt of documents or payment cheques/order books, etc. With computerized systems, there are usually inbuilt security devices which restrict access to the system and which also identify any individual who has done so in order to produce a payment of benefit.

Whatever the procedures, it is important that they record and reveal — at each stage of the process — precisely who had what part to play in the payment mechanism. Take as an example the payment process which results in an individual payment cheque being issued to a claimant. Batches of blank cheques — serially numbered — would be printed and issued to local offices, under strict security conditions and controls. At the local office level, each batch of cheques issued to clerical staff for preparation would be signed for. When handed to the next person involved in the production process, that individual would sign to acknowledge receipt ..... and so on, until the cheques were either posted (in which case the posting officer would give a signature to confirm that they *had* been posted) or handed personally to the beneficiary (who would sign to confirm receipt of the cheque). A similar series of receipts and acknowledgments would be necessary for *all* instruments of payment processed in the local office.

The security requirements begin, however, long before the preparation and issue stages of instruments of payment. When cheques and order books are being designed and printed it is important that every possible device is used to prevent them being copied or forged — in the same way that attempts are made to protect currency. In some countries, social security fraud is an enormous problem for the institution and everything possible must be done to prevent — or at least minimize — it.

There are many imaginative developments taking place around the world to make it impossible — or at least more difficult — for someone to obtain money, to which they are not entitled, from the social security institution. These include: the need to present personal identity documents at the time a benefit payment is collected or encashed; the use of "smart cards" to obtain payment; the increasing use of direct transfer of benefits into personal bank accounts, where such accounts are a common feature. Countries with poorly developed infrastructures or which do not yet have the advantage of well-developed, widespread, postal or banking facilities, often use methods such as fingerprinting, or membership identity cards bearing a photograph of the member, in an attempt to reduce the incidence of fraud and abuse.

In established schemes, the social security organization will normally include a number of personnel whose job it is to investigate cases of fraud — be it external or internal — but it is also important for the organization's operational departments always to be watchful of the need to tighten up security requirements whenever and wherever there are signs of weaknesses in procedures.

E. Audit and survey functions

Although reference to these functions is made in a section dealing with the award and payment of benefit, it should be noted that they apply equally to most other social security operations.

The internal audit function (which was dealt with comprehensively in Module 1, Unit 3D) is primarily concerned with matters of finance and security; the survey function is much more concerned with, and focuses on, the *procedures* followed by the organization.

Government auditing systems vary greatly from country to country with some having a totally independent auditing unit — for example a separate government department, a section of the finance ministry, treasury or revenue ministry, etc. However, as was also mentioned in the earlier unit, many of the larger social security institutions have their own "in-house" audit department which is responsible for auditing *all* the institution's financial activities. This would embrace an examination of the proper accounting for *all* monies received and paid by the institution, including contribution receipts, benefit payments, cash transactions, etc. In relation to benefit awards and payments, the functions of audit normally include the examination of benefit claims (usually a statistically based, random sample) to determine the level of accuracy of the awards and payments.

The survey function concentrates on organizational and procedural — rather than financial — aspects of the institution although, if incorrect payments or payment procedures come to light, the survey will of course draw attention to such errors. As with audit, there is usually an "in-house" department which is responsible for the survey function and its primary task is to continually monitor the institution's organization and procedures. The aim is not only to ensure that correct procedures are being followed but to develop, encourage and make known, "best practices" throughout the institution.

In-house survey teams are also able to provide advice on improved organization and methodology, and will often be able to identify gaps or weaknesses in procedures, gaps in knowledge, and perhaps consequential training needs. In some institutions, the survey function is a part of a wider "organization & method (O&M)" responsibility.

Audit and survey functions clearly demand very experienced personnel and it is usual to recruit staff internally, from those who have experience at "grass roots" level as well as from regional/headquarters levels. Some institutions require that auditing staff should have — or must obtain — accounting and/or auditing qualifications; although perhaps desirable, it is not as essential that they have extensive experience at local/regional level.

UNIT 3: Appeals procedures

A. *Rights of appeal and the appeals system*

Every claimant should have the right of appeal in the event that benefit is refused or where its quantity or quality is less than expected. This right is referred to in ILO Convention No. 102 (1952), although the Convention does not lay down any particular avenue of appeal or the process which is to be followed.

In some countries the normal courts of law are used; in others special social security tribunals are established; yet others use arrangements which exist under the labour legislation.

A later ILO Convention (No. 128, (1967)) requires that a claimant should have the right to be represented or assisted by a qualified person of his/her own choice, for example, by a delegate from a trade union. Although this Convention refers only to specific benefits (invalidity, old-age and survivors,) it is nevertheless usual to give the same rights of representation to all benefit cases.

Earlier reference was made to the need for decisions to be given by independent statutory authorities — in practice, nominated personnel in the social security institution — and for those decisions to be notified to claimants, whether favourable to the claimant or not. Most written communications which are issued to claimants — whether standard, mass-produced, printed forms, or individually prepared notifications or letters — contain information about appeal rights and the procedure for submitting an appeal.

Such notifications are basic to the appeals system, for it is perhaps the only way in which claimants might learn of their right of appeal. It therefore follows that any form or notification, which is to be used in connection with decisions on benefit claims, should include information about appeal rights and procedures.

Additionally, most social security institutions provide additional publicity — posters, leaflets, advertisements, etc. — to make members of the scheme aware of their appeal rights.

As with all other aspects of benefit procedures, it is important that the appeals system works efficiently and quickly. Those who claim benefit do so because they believe themselves to be entitled and will usually also be experiencing some loss or reduction of income because of the contingency which has prompted the claim. In the event that benefit is refused — or paid at a lower rate than was expected — a member will not wish to wait several months for an appeal to be processed. Having said that, the work involved in processing an appeal, constituting the appeal body and arranging a hearing, will inevitably take several weeks, even under the most efficient system. It follows, therefore, that *all* action resulting from the submission of an appeal must be *urgent* action.

It is usual to require that appeals are submitted in writing, normally within a prescribed period following receipt of the decision from the social security institution; 21 days is commonly used. The appeal can normally be lodged at any of the social security institution's offices but it is more common to require that it is sent to the office which issued the original decision. This enables the first stage of the appeal process to be taken promptly; that is, to re-examine the claim in order to ensure that the decision taken *was* correct. (Further reference will be made to this aspect in a later section which deals with "decisions and reviews".)

If, on re-examination, it is found that the original decision was *not* correct, it is usual to make a revised decision, notify the claimant and make any adjusting payment resulting from the revision. It should be remembered that the revised decision will also carry a right of appeal.

If the original decision *was* correct, then the appeal process will continue. This involves the preparation of a reference to the appeal body — the constitution of which will be dealt with in the following section — and the preparation and submission of documents to that body.

Some institutions have separate units or departments which deal with all stages of appeals, including preparation of documentation, arrangements for the hearing, constitution of the appeal body, etc. Other institutions may process the appeal at the local or perhaps regional/district level. As with many other organizational aspects, much will depend on the size of the institution, the country's infrastructural development, and the appeal system which has been adopted.

B. *The constitution of appeal tribunals*

Reference was made in the previous section to the variety of ways in which appeals are dealt with and to the fact that some schemes have special social security appeal bodies. These are often social security appeal tribunals having, as the title suggests, three members. Each tribunal is composed of a chairperson — usually legally qualified and often, for example, a local solicitor — and two members, representing employers and workers respectively. The two members are usually drawn from panels of employer and worker representatives. Workers' and employers' organizations are invited by the social security institution to submit a list of those of their members who are considered to be suitable for tribunal work; the lists of nominees will then be vetted, approved and drawn upon to constitute tribunals, as required.

The three tribunal members, in particular the chairperson, need to be familiar with the legislation governing the appeal cases which they will hear. Often the social security institution provides training in social security legislation for new tribunal members, soon after their first appointment.

It should be noted that the "balance" which is sought, by having employer *and* worker representatives on the tribunal, is not intended to produce a situation where one member is "for" or the other "against" the appellant (as the benefit claimant is now more correctly referred to). All three members are charged with considering all the facts of the case, the evidence before them, and the relevant legislation, and coming to a decision thereon. The tribunal favours neither the appellant nor the representative of the social security department. Both have equal status before the tribunal.

Fig. 18:
"... appellant ... and social security representative ... have equal status before the tribunal ..."

One other point should be noted about the constitution of tribunals and this relates to those cases which involve highly technical matters, in particular medical questions. Where the questions at issue relate, for example, to the degree of severity or the disabling effect of an illness, an accident at work or an industrial disease, it will often be necessary to have specialist appeal tribunals. These are sometimes referred to as "medical appeal tribunals". The procedures are very similar to other forms of tribunal but the chairperson and members are usually medically qualified.

C. Appeals procedure

Typically, the appeals procedure will follow a pattern similar to that described below.

On receipt of the letter of appeal (and following the re-examination of the claim referred to in Section A above) all the documents relating to the claim and the resulting decision will be passed to the clerk to the tribunal. The clerk will then be responsible for convening the tribunal, identifying a chairperson and two members — generally using a rota system to prevent the same people being used more often than is convenient for them. Copies of all relevant documents will then be issued to the appellant, to the tribunal members and to a representative of the social security department, together with a notice of the date, time and location of the tribunal hearing.

So far as possible, hearings are held locally in order to provide a greater opportunity for the appellant to attend in person. As pointed out previously, the appellant may choose to be represented and/or accompanied by "a qualified person of his own choice" and this will often be an official of the trade union or workers' association to which the appellant belongs.

Included in the papers submitted by the social security institution will be a reference to — and possibly an extract from — the appropriate legislation. The aim is to ensure that the tribunal — and the appellant — have *all* the relevant facts, information *and* legislation before them at the hearing, so that the tribunal's decision will take all factors into account.

It is worth re-emphasizing that the appellant and the social security representative have equal status before the tribunal, the tribunal members favouring neither but deciding purely on the information presented to them.

Despite having been provided with all the documentary information and evidence prior to the hearing, it is usual for the tribunal to give the appellant, his/her representative if present, and the social security representative, an opportunity to make a verbal presentation of their case. The tribunal members are also able to question those present.

The clerk, who although often an employee of the social security institution, adopts a totally neutral and impartial position at the hearing, indeed at all stages of the appeals process, and acts throughout simply as a servant of the tribunal ensuring, in particular, that hearings run smoothly.

When the chairperson is satisfied that the tribunal has obtained all relevant information, the appellant and the social security representative will be dismissed. The tribunal will then discuss and consider all the information and reach a decision. That decision may be unanimous or by majority and is normally notified to the appellant and the social security office in writing, by post, by the clerk to the tribunal.

Further rights of appeal, to a higher authority, exist in some countries and the overall procedures will be very similar to those already described. The main difference is that generally the higher the level of appeal, the more highly qualified will be the tribunal members. Some countries also provide for an ultimate right of appeal to be heard by their highest court of law.

The action following the appeal will of course depend on the decision given by the tribunal. If it is to confirm the original decision (given by the social security institution) there will be no need for further action, other than to notify the appellant (the claimant) that the tribunal has confirmed the original decision. If, however, the system provides for a further level of appeal, the appellant may decide to exercise the right to appeal to that higher level. In such a case a similar process would follow as was described for the initial appeal. The main difference, already referred to, is that the tribunal members would almost certainly be more highly qualified.

It should also be noted that if the tribunal gives a decision which changes the original decision of the social security institution, that institution also has a right of appeal against the tribunal's (revised) decision.

D. Decisions and reviews

Given the complexity of social security operations, the large volume of benefit claims, the need for speedy handling of claims, and the likelihood that claimants will not always produce all the necessary information or evidence, it is not surprising that misunderstandings and errors occur. It is therefore essential that remedies are available, within the administration, to correct wrong decisions or payments which have been made.

Often it will be the case that the original decision *was* made correctly, on the basis of the information available at the time (whether provided by the claimant or held within the social security institution) but that subsequent additional information sheds new light on the claim which, in turn, results in the need to change the original decision.

The administrative remedies will often include a formal procedure for review. Such a procedure enables a previous decision to be reviewed — re-examined — on receipt of additional information or evidence. Sometimes the result of the review will be to change the original decision — e.g. to pay rather than refuse benefit, or to pay at a higher (or perhaps even a lower) rate. Alternatively, the result of the review may be to confirm that the original decision was indeed correct. The review action will inevitably be followed by a further decision — to confirm, revise, or amend the original decision. As explained in an earlier unit, it is always necessary to formally notify the claimant (preferably in writing) of *any* decision taken on a claim. It therefore follows that a decision resulting from the review of an earlier decision should *also* be notified to the claimant. Normally this too would carry with it a further right of appeal for the claimant.

The facility to review usually applies not only to the adjudication officer who made the original decision, and to other adjudication officers within the local office which processed the claim, but also to adjudication officers at a higher level, e.g. at the institution's regional/provincial or headquarters offices.

Similarly, a decision given by an appeal tribunal effectively constitutes a new decision on a claim (or one or more aspects thereof) and will normally also carry a further right of appeal. However, a major difference in cases which go before an appeal tribunal is that (in many social security schemes) it is then open to *both* the claimant *and* the social security institution to appeal against the tribunal's decision.

It needs to be emphasized that the review procedures are first and foremost a vital and important safeguard for claimants. The aim is to ensure that each claim is dealt with strictly in accordance with the legislation, objectively and without fear or favour. The review procedures should therefore help to protect a claimant from any risk of refusal of benefit on "personal grounds" or at the whim of a member of the social security institution's staff.

This is yet another important reason for ensuring that each and every claim results in a formal — preferably written — notification to the claimant, explaining the decision made on that claim — even where the decision is totally favourable to the claimant. It also adds to the openness and transparency of the scheme to its members.

ADMINISTRATION OF SOCIAL SECURITY

MODULE 6:
PUBLIC RELATIONS

International Labour Office Geneva

MODULE CONTENTS

MODULE 6

PUBLIC RELATIONS

UNIT 1: What is meant by "public relations"?

Introduction

Public relations (PR) is a term which generally refers to the relationship between an organization and the community as a whole. One business dictionary defines PR as "a deliberate, planned and sustained effort to establish and maintain mutual understanding between an organization and its public". In our context, "PR" refers more specifically to the relationship between the social security institution and the contributors to/beneficiaries of the scheme. Occasionally there is some confusion between public relations and press or media relations and it should be remembered that these are simply two of many elements within the overall public relations activity.

It is essential to recognize that PR is as important a function for a government department, parastatal/non-governmental organization, *or* social security institution, as for any commercial enterprise.

Many of the larger social security institutions have their own public relations department; medium sized institutions often have a small group of specialist staff and even the smallest organizations usually have at least one member of staff who is given the responsibility for public relations activities, if only on a part-time basis. At the same time, it should not be forgotten that *all* staff in the institution — particularly those having regular contact with contributors and beneficiaries — have a part to play in and a contribution to make towards the overall PR activity.

It cannot be over-emphasized how important this administrative function is. It is vital that the organization recognizes the need for an active public relations component and that public relations work is approached in a proactive, rather than reactive way. This is especially important in the run-up to the introduction of any new scheme or prior to changes in an existing scheme. However, it is also important to realize that there is a *permanent* need for PR activity; it is not a need which becomes less important as schemes mature or which reduces with the passing of time. On the contrary, the need for effective PR increases over time and with each new development in a scheme.

There are many elements which contribute to a successful PR operation, one of which is the use of forms, posters and leaflets.

A. Forms, posters and leaflets

Forms

In the day to day administration of social security, there are so many situations which commonly apply to large numbers of contributors and beneficiaries that it becomes possible to produce a series of standardized communications to meet a range of needs. Such communications are usually referred to as "forms", and each one has its own unique purpose. In addition, many forms are produced by a social security institution for its own internal administrative use.

The design of forms is a challenging activity, for there are many conflicting demands. For the recipient, they must be clear and easy to understand, yet at the same time they must be legally correct and not open to misinterpretation or to misunderstanding. They need to be "customer friendly", not off-putting for the reader, yet they must at the same time retain an official style. This balance is not easy to achieve.

There is also a danger, when staff are issuing standardized forms, that they will be used with insufficient consideration for the recipient, for example through failing to make any modifications or amendments which are needed in order to make the form "fit" the particular circumstance. Some forms are specifically designed to obtain information and these often include a series of pre-printed questions. If the social security officer fails to delete those questions for which answers are already held, this not only gives a bad impression to the recipient but also makes it obvious that the form has been issued without much thought.

On a practical level, in order to distinguish between each of a series of forms and to facilitate ease of reference, printing arrangements, storage, identification, etc., each form should carry a unique number, perhaps combining an alphabetical prefix and a sequential number. For example, a series of forms used in connection with contribution activities may be a **CF** series (**C**ontribution **F**orm) and those used in connection with benefit procedures may be in a **BF** series (**B**enefit **F**orm). Forms used internally for personnel activities might carry a *Pers* prefix to the series and finance forms would perhaps use an *F* prefix.

Most administrations require that the issue of a form (whether internal or external) is recorded on the related papers, partly as a permanent record of action taken but also because of the possibility of subsequent enquiries.

All too often, when new forms are designed, insufficient attention is paid to their impact on recipients. Preoccupation with the institution's needs and objectives sometimes overshadows the potential effect on the public for whom they are intended.

Fig. 19:
"...possible to produce ... standardized communications ... forms ..."

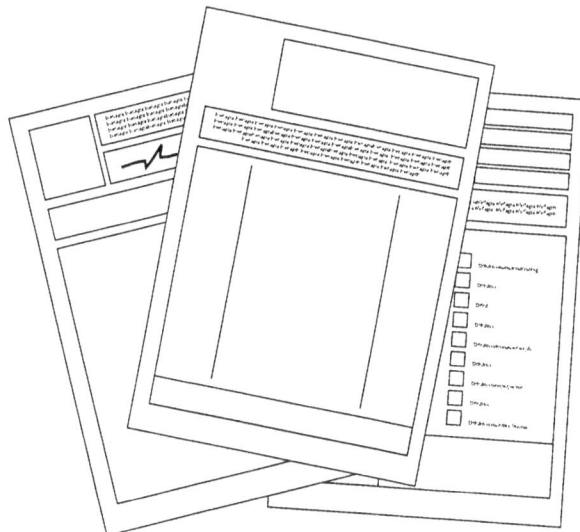

Posters

The dictionary definition suggests that a poster is a "placard containing information, displayed in a public place". The two key elements are "information" and "displayed in...public ..." but there is far more to a poster than simply the display of information.

The primary objective of any poster is to inform, and this clearly involves the need to ensure that it contains relevant information which can be quickly and easily understood. More than that, it needs to be displayed "... in a public place ..." but, more specifically, in a public place where the target population — primarily social security contributors and beneficiaries — is likely to see it. For example, a poster relating to maternity benefits and targeted at pregnant women may not be widely read or of much relevance if displayed in a geriatric hospital. Similarly, a poster relating to retirement benefits, targeting pensioners, might not be best placed in a children's clinic.

It is apparent, therefore, that although the design, layout and wording of a poster is of crucial importance, so also is the way in which it is used and the locations at which it is displayed.

Additionally, it is important that posters issued by the social security institution are immediately recognizable as being so. This often involves the use of logos, colour schemes and themes, etc., in order to enable the public to identify the source immediately.

Social security posters have to "compete" for attention with a variety of posters dealing with an enormous range of topics. They must therefore be able to attract — and hold — the attention of the reader, and succeed in transmitting the information.

Poster design may be one of the PR section's responsibilities, indeed, some of the larger institutions have their own graphic designers and reproduction unit; alternatively, smaller institutions may need to call upon the services of a design consultancy or publicity company. Whatever the arrangement, it is important that good quality posters are consistently used as part of the institution's effort to keep contributors and beneficiaries informed.

Leaflets

By "leaflet" is generally meant a small sheet or leaf of folded paper containing printed information; in the case of a social security institution, providing information relating to social security issues.

Large social security organizations produce an extensive range and variety of leaflets, covering almost every aspect of social security. A comprehensive series could well run to several hundred leaflets.

Fig. 20:
"... a range and variety of leaflets ..."

All the points made in earlier paragraphs, about the need for great care in designing and producing forms, apply equally to the design and production of social security leaflets. Leaflets need to be carefully targeted and well designed; the aim being to achieve clear and specific objectives. An important element of targeting is an awareness of the needs of the different groups to which information is directed. For example, a leaflet which is intended to provide information to individual workers about social security contribution rates and deductions will be very different to one which explains to employers how to remit the contributions deducted from workers. A leaflet explaining social security procedures to school leavers is likely to be quite different in its approach, language and tone to one which explains to widows the benefits they may be entitled to.

Leaflets are often much more understandable if they include visual illustrations as well as textual explanations. The language used in leaflets needs to be "simple and straight-forward", not technical, legal or complex. The use of jargon and officialese should be avoided. It must always be remembered that the aim is to provide the readers with information which they can understand and, often, instructions which they can follow. They should be clearer and better informed after reading the leaflet — not more confused.

Many social security institutions, which have members from different ethnic groups, produce leaflets in more than one language. For example, one European country has a range of leaflets in Arabic, Bengali, Chinese, Greek, Gujarati, Hindi, Punjabi, Somali, Turkish, Urdu and Vietnamese — in addition to the mother tongue.

Larger institutions may be in a position to create a professionally resourced unit or department for the design and production of leaflets, posters and forms. If the institution is too small to do so — or does not yet have adequate financial resources — it is useful to take professional advice from, or obtain the services of, a well-respected public relations company or publicity specialist.

It is impossible to over-estimate the value of well-produced forms, posters and leaflets, for they can make a major contribution to the level of knowledge, understanding and awareness of the scheme amongst contributors, beneficiaries and the public at large. Equally important is the enhancement of the institution's image and public profile.

B. The media

Newspapers, magazines, radio, television, professional journals, etc., can each, in their own way, play a significant part in the overall public relations activity of a social security institution. Each has its own particular advantages and disadvantages, and these always need to be carefully weighed. No single medium will achieve all that is required by way of the institution's total public relations effort. That will best be achieved by a carefully considered, well balanced mix, with each being used to its best advantage.

Most institutions will, at one time or another, receive a "bad press" and these are the times when a prompt and effective response is required. Such responses are necessarily reactive and are an inevitable part of a social security institution's relations with the public. However, it is vital that the main thrust of public relations work is based on a proactive approach to the media.

Whether it be at national level, with the national media, or at provincial or local levels with their respective media, it is always good policy to work in close cooperation and establish positive and constructive working relationships. If each level of the institution can operate very openly with its media contacts — whilst paying due regard to the need for confidentiality on individual cases — it is less likely that there will be sustained criticism of the scheme's operations.

Newspapers, magazines, journals

Many newspapers and magazines carry some form of "complaints column" or "enquiry hotline" for readers and these often attract their fair share of items about social security issues. A close working relationship with newspaper and magazine publishers will often encourage them to check out readers' complaints with the local social security office *before* going into print. This not only gives an opportunity for the office to remedy any errors which may have been made but also provides an opportunity to the newspaper or magazine to sift out any complaints which may have been made maliciously, which are exaggerated, or which are factually incorrect.

Where a poor working relationship exists between a newspaper and the institution there is a likelihood that any or all complaints received by the paper will be published, regardless of their accuracy or legitimacy.

Bearing in mind the earlier reference to proactive public relations, newspapers and magazines can be useful vehicles for informing and educating the public. Some social security institutions have an arrangement with newspapers and other publications to feature a series of weekly or monthly articles, each one focusing on a particular aspect of the social security scheme, for example one of the scheme's benefits — how to claim, what the conditions are, what is payable, how payments are made, etc. This facility can also be of great help at times when major changes are taking place in a scheme, for example when new benefits are being introduced or when social security legislation is being amended.

Television

In countries where television transmissions are widely received, and where the majority of homes have a television receiver, the medium can be a valuable one through which to inform and educate. This may be by using advertising slots (where there is a commercial channel) or through news and current affairs programmes. The impact will be far greater if social security items can be screened immediately before or after a peak viewing programme, given that the optimum number of viewers is likely to be reached at such a time. Television will clearly not be as useful, however, where very few households — perhaps only the most prosperous — have receivers. In such a situation, any transmission — including those relating to social security issues — will reach only a relatively small proportion of the population, which may well mainly include those with little interest in or need for social security information.

Radio

In many countries, especially developing countries, it is far more likely that radio — be it local or national — will reach more people than either television or newspapers. Countries in development often find that, whilst newspaper circulation tends to be centred on the capital or a few major towns, radios are much more widely available, even in very remote areas. The very poorest countries often have quite widespread ownership of, or communal access to, radios. The development of "clockwork mechanism" radio receivers, which operate without electricity or battery cells, should ultimately make the medium even more widely available. The fact that literacy is not a requirement for listening to radio, together with other factors already mentioned, means that radio is an excellent medium for spreading information on a range of issues, including social security, to large numbers of the population over vast areas of the country.

As with regular television broadcasts, it is beneficial to have a regular "slot" which listeners can expect at a set time on a fixed day. By so doing, the potential size of the listening audience is increased, the more so if that slot can be — as for television — one side or the other of a peak audience programme.

Contacts with the media

The importance of maintaining good working relationships with the media cannot be over-emphasized. It is important that contact personnel in the media are supportive and that positive, constructive steps are taken by the social security institution — at each of its organizational levels — to ensure that those contacts become allies rather than adversaries. This is not to say that the institution should be prepared to go to any lengths to court favour with the media or pay any price to please them. It is essential that the social security institution maintains very high standards, upholds the highest principles and, at all times, acts with integrity and dignity in its dealings with the media. For example, care must be taken to avoid revealing confidential information — whether deliberately or accidentally — about individual cases, and care must also be taken to check sources of information before responding to criticism or complaints. It is important to ensure that media representatives are not provided with information which they should not be in possession of, for example "off the record", or confidential information about individual beneficiaries or contributors. In short, the public at large must be confident that the vast amount of confidential information held by the institution is secure, that it can be trusted to safeguard such information, and that it will not reveal *any* information of a confidential or personal nature to third parties.

It is only by achieving and maintaining such a level of trust that the institution will earn the respect of the public it is there to serve.

C. Advertising

A social security institution, like all other organizations in the public and private sectors, needs to make use of advertising. Perhaps the only significant difference is that a social security institution does not advertise in order to sell a product; it advertises primarily to educate or inform.

Although advertising will usually be an ongoing activity, there are times when widespread advertising campaigns are a particularly useful form of public relations vehicle. The introduction of a new social security scheme; major changes, modifications or additions to an existing scheme; changes in contribution or benefit rates and revised claims procedures are just a few examples of situations which might benefit from a well-planned advertising campaign.

The points made in previous sections about choosing the most appropriate medium — newspapers, magazines, radio, television, etc. — apply equally to considerations about advertising. The objective is clearly for advertisements to reach as many people as possible and, to that end, they should be placed wherever they will help achieve that objective.

In addition to the more obvious placements — newspapers, publications, radio, television, etc. — there are other potentially useful, though perhaps less obvious, locations. Commercial advertising hoardings, public transport advertising display panels, community centre notice boards, and the like, are some of the many locations which have the potential to reach those who need the information.

As with all the public relations activities already examined in this unit, it is necessary to be imaginative and inventive in the use of advertising, whilst at the same time not losing sight of the purpose — to inform or educate contributors, beneficiaries or the public at large.

UNIT 2: Proactive approaches

A. Information campaigns

The point was made previously that it is important to adopt a proactive approach to the media as part of the institution's public relations activities. However, the media is but one of many avenues which are available to the institution for the dissemination of information about social security issues.

Information campaigns are particularly appropriate at times of major developments in a social security scheme. The initial launch of a new scheme, or a major extension or change to an existing scheme, are examples of occasions when a fully co-ordinated public information campaign might well be appropriate.

Such a campaign will involve most, if not all, the public relations resources referred to already: press, radio, TV, advertising, etc. Additionally it may also need to be augmented by talks and presentations to a wide range of organizations — including trade unions, employers, associations, pressure groups, special interest groups and many others — at all levels, national, provincial, and local.

Campaigns of this kind must be very carefully planned, well designed, highly developed and fully co-ordinated. It is essential that all those involved in the delivery of any part of the campaign are fully informed and properly trained in order to play their part and make their contribution successfully. It is also important to ensure that *all* the social security institution's staff are aware of the campaign and its objectives in order that they are prepared for enquiries which may be prompted from members of the public.

A successful information campaign is likely to do much more than achieve its primary objective — to inform and educate. It will also provide an opportunity to favourably impress contributors and beneficiaries and raise confidence in the institution amongst the public at large.

B. *Help Desks*

Help Desks are another proactive way of reaching members of the public, especially at the local level. They can be located almost anywhere but are most usefully located in public places which attract large numbers of people. Shopping malls, local markets, libraries, community centres, village halls, local hospital reception areas, exhibition centres, bus or train station forecourts, waiting areas, country fairs, are just a few examples of venues which can provide a suitable location for a Help Desk and thereby provide yet another contact point between the staff of the social security institution and members of the public.

Some Help Desk locations may be a permanent feature but, more commonly, they are a temporary, short-term facility which can be set up using very little equipment. Often all that is required is one or two knowledgeable and experienced members of the local social security office staff, a table and chairs, a display board with posters and a supply of the more frequently used leaflets. This is a very convenient method of taking a social security information point to "members of the public", which of course embodies beneficiaries and contributors, and has the potential to play a very useful part in the institution's service to the public.

One important feature of Help Desks is that they are on "neutral ground" and this is often helpful to anyone who is, for whatever reason, reluctant to visit a local social security office.

Some social security institutions have developed this concept and further extended the facility by providing mobile information units. These may be purpose-built vehicles — virtually a mobile miniature social security public caller office — or simply a car or van carrying a small supply of leaflets. These mobile units move around from village to village, on fixed days, during set times, and are particularly useful contact points for those who are unable to travel and who may have no other means of contacting the office.

If the social security office cannot justify or afford its own mobile unit, it may be possible to utilize other existing mobile services — for example mobile libraries, clinics, etc. It is also sometimes possible to arrange with those services to share vehicles, perhaps on a cost-sharing basis.

This brief reference to some of the ways in which information and help can be taken out into the community illustrates the need for imaginative and innovative thinking to meet the challenge of keeping the public informed.

Fig. 22:
"... Help Desks ... a temporary ... facility ... using very little equipment ..."

C. In-house publications

In-house publications are the internal publications produced with the aim of keeping the organization's staff fully informed about its activities. Sometimes referred to as "house magazines" or "house journals", such publications can make an important contribution towards keeping staff up to date with the changes and developments taking place within the institution.

In the larger social security institutions, many of the staff will be trained to specialize on relatively narrow activities, for example processing a particular benefit, checking or recording contribution remittances, dealing with routine enquiries, etc. Consequently, staff may find it difficult to keep abreast of developments in those parts of the organization beyond their immediate sphere of operations. It is particularly important, therefore, that efforts are made to keep all staff regularly informed about what the institution is doing — including making them aware of public relations activities. Local staff, in particular, are in the forefront of day-to-day contact with the public and it is clearly essential that they be kept well informed. Internal circulars and house journals can play an important part in doing so, even though they have their limitations.

Beyond the immediate objective of keeping staff up to date and well informed, however, in-house publications can make a major contribution to raising and sustaining staff morale. In addition to informative items about the institution's work it is often beneficial to include items of personal interest: for example, about individual members of staff; activities undertaken or special achievements made by particular offices, departments, or sections; initiatives developed by individuals or groups within the institution, etc.

In-house publications range from very basic, inexpensive, internal productions to printed publications produced externally by commercial printing companies. In the latter case, they can be expensive but that need not always be a disincentive for the organization as many such publications carry commercial advertisements, the revenue from which may cover publication and distribution costs.

D. The role of staff training in public relations

The training of the social security institution's staff has both a direct and indirect impact on its public relations activities. A substantial proportion of the staff of any social security organization will be engaged on duties which involve regular contact with contributors, beneficiaries or members of the general public. Whether that contact is face to face, over the telephone or through written communication it is nevertheless a crucial part of the day-to-day, ongoing public relations work of the institution.

Any form of training which staff undertake in order to perform their work — whether that training be basic induction, job-training, technical or specialist training — will have some bearing on their future dealings with members of the public. Indirectly, therefore, all training provided by the institution has a potential for influencing the way in which staff relate to the public.

There are also many forms of training to be given which will have a direct and positive impact on the public relations activities of the institution. Social security institutions with well developed in-house training programmes include, in their regular series of in-house courses, training on "Service to the public" for front-line staff. This form of training generally includes, for example, interviewing skills and techniques; letter writing; correct use of the telephone; and sometimes "specialist" skills such as dealing with the recently bereaved. The training may be given on courses which are designed specifically to deal with those topics or may be included in technical, procedural or job-training courses.

Reference has already been made to the part which talks and presentations to external groups, by members of the institution's staff, can play in the overall public relations context. Speaking to an audience demands certain techniques, skills and abilities, which few people have naturally but which most people can be trained to develop. It is therefore possible to enhance the quality of external presentations by providing training in "public speaking" to those of the institution's staff who will be faced with this task. Large social security organizations should be able to include such training in their in-house programmes, using in-house staff trainers; smaller ones may need to use external training providers.

One of the most serious mistakes that any social security organization can make, in its overall approach to public relations activities, is to overlook or under-estimate the part which training needs to play. Providing training for social security staff, in effective service to the public whom they are there to serve, is not a luxury — it is a necessity. Such training needs to be ongoing — not "one off". If training is inadequate, the quality of public relations work will be adversely affected. Whilst it does not automatically follow that provision of effective training guarantees the highest standard of public relations, it cannot help but improve its quality.

As with all other aspects of the public relations effort, the training of staff must be based on a proactive approach. In practice this means that, in addition to the ongoing regular training of staff, training should also be given in anticipation of a particular need, to prevent or minimize the possibility of a public relations disaster. Training which is *prompted* by such a disaster is reactive and usually much too late.

ADMINISTRATION OF SOCIAL SECURITY

MODULE 7: MANAGEMENT OF SOCIAL SECURITY INSTITUTIONS

International Labour Office Geneva

MODULE CONTENTS

MODULE 7

MANAGEMENT OF SOCIAL SECURITY INSTITUTIONS

UNIT 1: Managing human resources

Introduction

The second half of the twentieth century has seen an enormous expansion of literature on "management". The range and variety of approaches is so great as to defy any simple grouping or system of classification into "schools of thought". In the introductory module to this manual, the point was made that principles of management are quite unlike the principles of mathematics or the laws of the natural sciences.

The management of a social security organization is little — if at all — different from the management of any other organization, institution or enterprise, whether public or private. Indeed, social security *is* an enterprise and, in many cases, one of the most important in the country.

With these comments in mind, it will be apparent that this module dealing with "management of social security institutions" can do little more than draw attention to and briefly comment upon some of the more important features of management in such an institution.

Throughout the units referring to human resource issues, it should constantly be born in mind that "human resources" means people, and that people in any organization have individual needs and aspirations.

It is therefore incumbent on social security managers — at all levels — to be constantly searching for ways of improving and extending collective and individual job satisfaction. Also, of ensuring fair and equitable treatment for all personnel, for example, by adopting transparent and impartial recruitment and promotion procedures, by reaching collective agreements with staff on pay and conditions, which are comprehensive in scope and which are fully honoured. Mutual respect between the management and staff of the institution is one of the keys to a successful administration.

A. Evaluation of staffing requirements

In a world of rapidly changing technology, with an ever-growing demand for more and different skills, the need to plan manpower — human resources — is as great as the need to plan any other resource.

The development and success of any organization rests, in the final analysis, on the quality of its human resources and the extent to which their talents and abilities are used to the full.

Manpower planning is concerned with safeguarding the future and is an integral part of an organization's forward planning. It is not a separate, esoteric activity carried out by a few people, at the top of the organization, simply by pulling numbers out of a hat. It is, or should be, part of the regular, ongoing, conduct of business in all organizations.

The need for organizations to take a searching look at manpower requirements has become increasingly important, not least because of ever-increasing manpower costs. An organization contemplating the purchase of an expensive piece of machinery or equipment would do so most carefully, having regard to its suitability for the purpose for which it was intended, its capacity, the means by which that capacity could be utilized to the full, its place in the scheme of production and the expected return on the investment. Few organizations, however, apply the same level of consideration to manpower.

One reason for this difference in approach lies in the traditional attitude to manpower as a cost rather than as an investment. Yet while machinery and equipment depreciates and eventually becomes obsolete, well-developed manpower will usually continue to grow in usefulness, capacity and value.

Forecasting manpower requirements depends on the data on which it is based and the judgement of those involved in the forecasting. However, it is clearly very difficult to make an accurate forecast of the manpower which will be required by a newly established social security institution, particularly because such data will not yet be available. At the planning phase, the initial manpower requirements may need to be simply a best estimate, based on the anticipated work loads of each part of the new organization. At this stage, it may be helpful to have regard to staffing levels and staff ratios (clerical to supervisory to managerial personnel) in similar institutions.

There is a fine and difficult balance to be struck at this initial stage. Recruiting more staff than required may result in long-term over-manning problems, under-employment, reduced output levels and difficulties of adjusting (in particular, reducing) staff numbers. Under-recruitment will almost certainly adversely affect the processing times and the speed with which contributors and beneficiaries are dealt with and is therefore likely to lead to complaints and enquiries — which in turn will add to the workload and to a further increase of arrears. In this crucial phase of development, the last thing the new institution needs is a poor public image and signs of incompetence.

As the organization progresses to a fully operational level, statistics, data, information on processing and clearance times will increasingly become available and will enable much more accurate revisions of the early estimates and consequential adjustments of manpower levels.

The objective of manpower planning is — and must always be — to improve manpower utilization and to ensure that there is available manpower, of the right number and the right quality, to meet the present and future needs of the organization. The institution must therefore develop a realistic recruitment policy, and recruitment plan, and be greatly concerned with manpower costs and productivity.

B. *Recruitment and selection*

The aim of *recruitment* is to ensure that the organization's demand for manpower is met, by attracting potential employees (recruits) in a cost-effective and timely manner. The aim of *selection* is to identify, from those coming forward and presenting themselves for recruitment, the individuals who appear most likely to fulfil the requirements of the organization. The recruitment activities of an organization are generally carried out by the staff of the Personnel Department.

Before looking at some of the policies and procedures relating to recruitment and selection, it is appropriate to remember that the recruitment process even has a part to play in the public relations policy of the social security institution. The projection of the institution's corporate image is reinforced not only through the job advertisement but even more so in the handling of candidate response by the "recruiters" (usually the staff of the Personnel Department). People who are treated well when they seek employment with the institution are potential ambassadors for that institution — whether or not they are successful in their application. Conversely, those who are treated badly during the recruitment process will probably be quick to spread their criticism. Examples of bad treatment include: not acknowledging letters of application; failing to notify individuals of the results of their application; keeping them waiting for an interview; failing to inform unsuccessful applicants of the outcome of an interview.

It is therefore wise to remember that the *quality* of the institution's recruitment procedures may have a far wider impact than might be expected.

Recruitment

Recruitment policies constitute the code of conduct which the organization is prepared to follow in its search for possible recruits in the market-place. A specific policy will need to be developed by each individual organization but it may be useful to provide an illustration of some of the features which a reputable policy might embrace.

In matters of recruitment, the organization *will:*

- advertise all vacancies internally before making use of external sources;

- always advertise under the organization's name when advertising externally;

- ensure that each applicant for a position in the organization is informed in advance of the basic details of the vacancy and the basic conditions of employment attached to it;

- ensure that applicants are kept informed of their progress, throughout the recruitment procedures;

- seek possible candidates on the basis of their ability and suitability to perform the job required.

In matters of recruitment, the organization *will not:*

- make exaggerated or misleading claims in recruitment literature or job advertisements;

- discriminate unfairly against possible candidates on the grounds of sex, race, religion or physical disability.

Another essential requirement of the organization's recruitment policy and procedures is that they must be open and transparent. This is vital for any organization but is particularly relevant where there is a history or culture of direct recruitment — as is the case in some developing countries — without advertisement or competition, of relatives, friends or others on a personal basis. Equally damaging to an institution's reputation is any suggestion that sinecures are being dispensed. Such practices are guaranteed to harm the institution's external image and reputation, to have a negative effect on the morale of its staff, weaken the internal management and reduce the operational ability of the institution.

Limitations of space prevent more than a brief overview of recruitment procedures. Nevertheless, it is possible to point to some of the considerations which need to be applied in order to ensure a rational and logical approach to the recruitment of new employees.

A well organized Personnel Department will make use of some form of checklist to help minimize errors and omissions in the recruitment process. Such a checklist would contain — as a minimum — the following questions for consideration:

- Has/have the vacancy/vacancies been agreed by the responsible manager?

- Is there an up-to-date job description for each vacant position?

- What are the conditions of employment (salary, hours, holidays, etc.) for the position?

- Has a "candidate specification" been prepared?

- Has a notice of the vacancy been circulated internally?

- Do all potential candidates — internal and external — know where to apply and in what form (letter, application form, etc.)?

- What arrangements have been drawn up for shortlisting candidates?

- Have the interview arrangements been agreed: have shortlisted candidates been informed?

- Have unsuitable candidates or "reserves" been informed of their position?

- Have offer of appointment letters been agreed and despatched to successful candidates? Have references been taken up, where necessary?

- Have suitable rejection letters been sent to unsuccessful shortlisted candidates, thanking them for their attendance?

For successful candidates:

- Have all replies to offer of appointment letters been accounted for?

- Have the necessary procedures for placement, induction and follow up of successful candidates been put into effect?

At this point a comment about external advertisements is appropriate. These will usually be placed in the press and/or in professional journals, depending on the level of the vacancy being advertised. An effective job advertisement (i.e. one that attracts sufficient numbers of the right kind of candidates) should, ideally, contain the features listed below.

It should:

- provide brief but succinct details about the position to be filled;

- provide similar details about the employing/recruiting organization;

- provide details of all *essential* personal requirements, including specific academic qualifications where these are required;

- make reference to any *desirable* personal qualities or requirements;

- state the main conditions of employment, including an indication of the salary for the position;

- make clear to whom the application or enquiry should be directed.

It is also important to present the information contained in the advertisement in an attractive form, not only with a view to gaining the attention of potential candidates but also because — as mentioned earlier in this section — it has a part to play in, and a contribution to make towards, the overall public relations image of the organization.

Selection

Recruitment's task is to locate possible applicants and attract them to the organization. Selection activities are designed, firstly, to identify those candidates who, on the evidence available, appear to be the most suitable for the vacancies to be filled; secondly, to persuade those candidates to join the organization by making acceptable offers of employment to them.

Most social security institutions, like many other public and private enterprises, now insist on minimum academic qualifications at each level of intake, with clerical grades and/or junior posts requiring relatively basic educational qualifications and the most senior posts demanding degrees and/or advanced professional qualifications. Normally the only personnel likely to be recruited without the need for academic qualifications are the support staff — messengers, drivers, gardeners, cleaners, perhaps security guards, etc.

Selection activities are dominated by application procedures and interviews. Letters or forms of application provide the basic information of the selection process and this is built on by means of interviews, tests and references.

The most widely used technique in the selection process is the interview. Well behind the interview, in terms of popularity, comes psychological testing, often referred to as selection tests. These include intelligence tests, aptitude tests, attainment tests and personality tests.

An effective interview should produce a lively and relevant exchange of information between interviewer(s) and candidate, which enables both parties to make up their minds about each other. The achievement of this situation depends mainly on the competence of interviewers in terms of how well prepared they are and how well they handle the progress of the interview.

Interviews which are conducted on a one-to-one or two-to-one basis can normally be expected to more easily facilitate a flow of information between candidate and interviewer(s). Panel interviews, where three or more people may be facing the candidate, are an altogether more formal affair and may restrict or reduce the flow of information between the two sides.

Tests are used by some organizations, as part of the selection process, as they can provide useful information which adds to, or confirms, other information arising from the application form or interview. However, if used, it is essential that they are well organized and used with great care.

Limitations of space permit only brief reference to some of the key aspects of recruitment and selection. However, as a final comment on the topic, it is worth remembering that the principle of "... do unto others as you would be done by ..." should underpin the whole of the recruitment and selection procedure. The job applicant, at whatever level, expects to receive the normal human courtesies, not only in the face-to-face situation but at all other points of contact during the recruitment and selection process. It follows, therefore, that a great deal of attention must be placed on the underlying social processes.

C. Training

People are the main resource in all organizations. If they are not appropriately trained for the work they have to perform they will not do it as efficiently or as effectively as they could. It then follows that the operations of the organization will not be as successful as would otherwise be the case. In a social security institution, the result is that contributors and beneficiaries are unlikely to receive the service to which they are entitled and which they have a right to expect.

Training can be distinguished from education and development as follows:

* *Training* is concerned with imparting knowledge and improving skills *in relation to a job or occupation* ... whereas *education* is part of a personal *preparation for life* and ... *development*, so far as the work setting is concerned, is aimed at personal growth and *realization of potential* as an employee.

There are many organizations which do not consider training to be sufficiently central to their operations for it to be one of the main components of their corporate strategy. Regrettably, many social security institutions also adopt this view. Even where such institutions *do* recognize the need for training, it is often a vulnerable area for, when times are hard or budgets are being squeezed, it is often training programmes that are among the first to suffer cutbacks. Training budgets are also vulnerable because training is often regarded as an optional extra.

"Systematic training" is the term used to describe a rational approach to training and development based on the following:

* a training policy

* a training organization

* the identification of training needs (sometimes referred to as "Training Needs Analysis" — TNA)

* the planning and execution of training

* the evaluation of training.

Each plays an important part in the overall training effort and is worthy of individual comment.

Fig. 23:
"Each plays an important part in the overall training effort ..."

The training policy

In some cases this may be no more than a general statement that "the organization will provide resources to ensure that key skills are maintained ...". In other cases, the policy may be much more detailed, perhaps referring comprehensively to the various actions to be taken to ensure both a regular supply of skills and a high degree of personal motivation, through development opportunities provided by the organization.

However it is stated or defined, it is vital for the organization's success that the policy demands on-going, rather than stop-start, programmes for the training of staff.

These programmes should recognize the need for training of staff at *all* levels of the organization. Too often the mistake is made of concentrating the majority of the training effort — and expenditure — on small numbers of senior personnel. Another frequent failing is to focus too heavily on external training (which is usually expensive, relative to the training budget) rather than on in-house training. What is required is a good balance between the two.

The training organization

In the smaller institutions, the responsibility for training will usually be one of the many functions of the Personnel Department. Larger institutions often have a permanent training unit, staffed with a team of training officers and administrative staff. The way in which training is organized and delivered will clearly also be influenced by the size of the institution. Nevertheless, all training organizations have similar responsibilities and commitments. These include the responsibility for identifying training needs, designing programmes to meet those needs, delivering in-house training activities or courses to provide the knowledge and skills required and, in some cases, arranging for attendance on external courses to meet part of the training needs.

In-house programmes often include "off the peg" training courses (those which are repeated at regular intervals to meet a recurring need of the organization) and "tailor-made" courses (those which are designed to meet a one-off or infrequent need).

Identifying training needs

Those responsible for training must, first of all, establish what the training needs of the organization are. It is important to recognize that the identification of training needs is *not* a one-off exercise; it is an on-going activity, part of a continuous process aimed at ensuring that the organization's training delivery matches its training requirements.

If the task of identifying training needs is to be undertaken seriously (and it is a sad fact that many organizations fail to make any attempt to assess their training needs), it should make use of all available sources of information. There are two main approaches to identifying needs. The first is to look at the operational efficiency of the organization; the second looks at the training needs of individuals. It is important, however, to use *both* approaches in order to obtain a comprehensive picture of the organization's training needs.

Operational needs

In considering operational efficiency, it will be useful to identify any jobs within the organization which appear to be holding back the achievement of satisfactory levels of performance and which training may improve. Note should also be taken of indicators of accuracy, clearance times and output levels, for these may highlight aspects of the work which training could improve. Inadequate training can be one of the many contributing factors to low staff morale; where morale is low, therefore, it is wise to consider whether training can play a part in raising the level. Information may be available from the findings in audit and survey reports which could indicate a training need. Discussions with managers and supervisors will often help identify training needs which are common to several staff or departments. The personal experience and knowledge of the training officer(s) will also contribute to the process of identifying needs. One important source of suggestions for training activities which should not be overlooked — but often is — is the staff themselves. Who better to say what is required to help them do their job better than those who are doing the work?

Individual needs

The second approach, that of identifying *individual* training needs, also has a number of potentially useful sources. Amongst these are individual job descriptions, personnel specifications, communication needs, and level and quality of service to the public. On a more personal level, the information about particular individuals which is available (from performance assessments, reports of appraisal interviews, notes made at counselling interviews, personal training records, etc.) often provides a useful guide to their individual training needs.

Fig. 24:
"... identifying training needs ..."

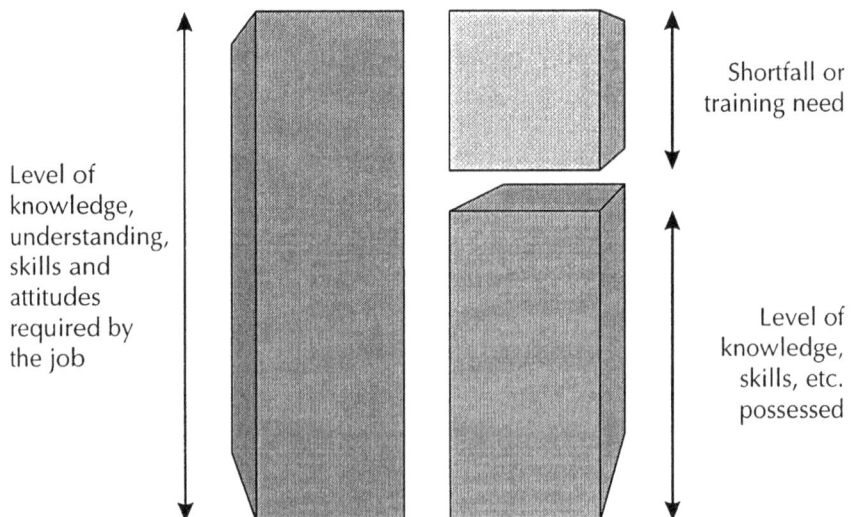

Level of knowledge, understanding, skills and attitudes required by the job

Shortfall or training need

Level of knowledge, skills, etc. possessed

Without seeking to pre-judge what the results of a training needs assessment process would reveal, it can reasonably be expected to include some or all of the following training requirements:

- induction training —
  for new staff, or existing staff moving to a different department;

- basic, on-the-job training -
  in technical and procedural aspects;

- communications and "service to the public" training —
  for all staff who have contact with the public, whether face-to-face, by telephone or via written communications;

- specialist training —
  for staff undertaking special tasks or needing special skills (e.g. compliance officers, fraud officers, adjudication officers, etc.);

- supervisory training —
  for those who have a responsibility for supervising staff;*

- management training —
  for those in managerial positions;#

- public relations -
  for staff involved in PR activities;#

---

* Smaller social security institutions may need to use external training providers for some or all of this.

Even the larger institutions may need to use external providers for some or all of this.

Planning the training

Once the training needs have been identified, the training unit will then have to sort out the training priorities, draw up the initial training plans and (in most organizations) have them approved by senior management. The plan should spell out the key areas for training, numbers and categories of staff to be trained, preliminary time-tabling of the training programmes included in the plan and, where appropriate, the costs which will be incurred.

The training plan should encompass:

- *what* training is to be provided

- *how* it is to be provided

- *when* it is to be provided

- by *whom* it is to be provided

- *where* it is to be provided

- *at what cost* it is to be provided.

Implementation of the training programme

All that then remains to be done is to *implement* the programme of training. However, this is perhaps the stage where the process is most easily blown off course. Far too often training programmes are interrupted, suspended, halted or even terminated, because of "more urgent demands" on trainees or trainers. Regrettably, in many cases this is simply an easy way of solving an organizational or staffing problem and one indicator of the importance which an institution attaches to training is its readiness — or reluctance — to interfere with planned training activities.

At this point it is appropriate to refer to one particular training method which plays a major part in any organization's training activities — "on-the-job" training. This often takes place at the desk and is, therefore, widely referred to as "desk training". It is usually provided by an experienced colleague or member of the section/department in which the trainee works.

Desk training can play a valuable part in the overall training effort — provided that the individual who is giving the training is an *effective* trainer. All too often, insufficient thought or preparation is given to this form of training. Even though the trainer may be a very experienced, very quick, and very accurate worker, it does not always or necessarily follow that he/she will be the most effective trainer. It should be remembered, therefore, that desk-trainers need to be carefully chosen, with as much importance being attached to their suitability as a trainer as to their technical knowledge. It should also be recognized that they themselves may need some training in "how to train". This requirement for "trainer training" becomes yet another of the organization's training needs; indeed it must be an *integral* part of the organization's training programme.

Before moving on to the last operational stage in the training process — validation and evaluation — it should be noted that the process does not end there, for this is a cyclical series of activities, as illustrated by Figure 25.

Fig. 25:
Systematic training: the basic cycle

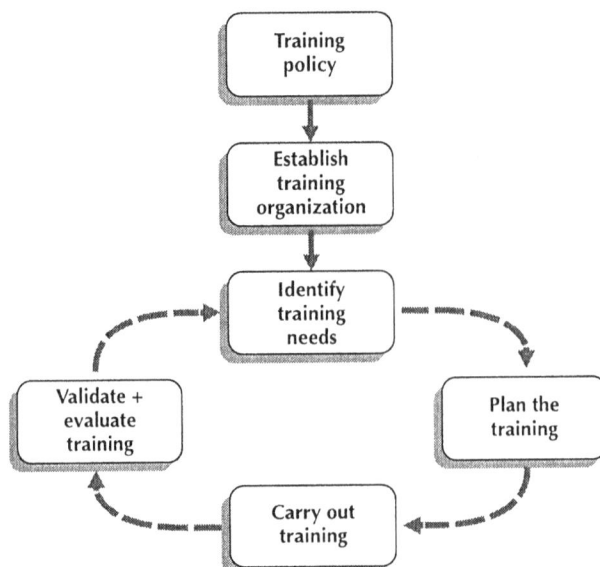

- Training policy
- Establish training organization
- Identify training needs
- Plan the training
- Carry out training
- Validate + evaluate training

Validating and evaluating the training

Training *evaluation* is concerned with the financial and social effectiveness of training, taking into account the cost-effectiveness and cost-benefit analysis. Training *validation* looks at how effective the training was in relation to pre- and post-training levels of knowledge or skills. Evaluation and validation are terms which tend to be used interchangeably and which are sometimes confused one with the other. They represent a stage in the overall training operation which is often dealt with unsatisfactorily — if at all.

The starting point is to compare the results achieved by the training with the original training objectives and, where possible, measure the degree of improvement. Although this can be done fairly easily for some training activities, it is extremely difficult with others. On the one hand, for example, training in keyboard skills enables quite precise measurements of speed and accuracy before and after a training activity. On the other hand, any training which involves attitudes, concepts, supervisory or management skills, is difficult — if not impossible — to quantify. Any attempt to measure the achievements of such training will, at best, be based on subjective assessment.

Having pointed to some of the difficulties, it nevertheless needs to be recognized that it *is* important to build into the overall training process some form of validation procedure. A variety of methods and approaches are available, ranging from the quantifiable (the keyboarding example) to the subjective, e.g. completion of individual "feedback" questionnaires at the end of a training course. In addition, feedback is available from a number of other sources. Appraisal interviews may provide comments on, and an indication of the value of, the training received by a member of staff. The job performance, following a period of training, ought to give some indication of whether or not the training achieved its objectives. It is useful, therefore, to obtain comments from supervisors and linemanagers shortly after a member of their team returns from a training activity.

Increasingly, validation and evaluation procedures are being developed which provide more objective and accurate measurement of training achievements. Some of these are being adopted by organizations which have substantial training commitments and large training units. For most institutions, however, it is sufficient that *some* organized attempt is made to validate and evaluate training, even where that attempt tends to be subjective and imperfect. It is far better to undertake *some* validation/evaluation — even if not entirely successfully — than none at all.

The validation/evaluation stage completes the cycle of training activities which was referred to earlier in the section.

However, that cycle must now begin again (see Figure 25) because the results of the validation and evaluation will become part of the revised training needs which may, in turn, lead to a revision of the training plan, to further training, followed by more evaluation, etc.

If that cycle stops, there is a risk of the training programme becoming static and stale rather than keeping abreast — and preferably ahead — of the organization's training needs.

D. Staff reporting and appraisal

The two terms are often used interchangeably but there is a very clear distinction to be made between them, for each has a different, albeit related, objective.

Staff reports

Staff reports, which in most organizations are completed annually, serve a number of useful purposes:

- they provide a continuous (year-on-year) record of performance by which an individual's progress can be judged;

- they indicate the capacity to perform the present job and show how well or badly each part of that job was done;

- they indicate the suitability for other jobs within the organization;

- they provide information which will be helpful when selection for promotion is being considered;

- they are a useful source of information in general personnel matters, e.g. efficiency, training, conduct, etc.;

- in aggregate, a batch of reports on a group of staff in a particular section, department or branch will be helpful in presenting a picture of the prevailing staff standards therein.

Given the potential value of reports, as summarized above, it is important that they should be as informative and comprehensive as possible and it is absolutely essential that they are completed objectively and impartially. Those requirements are far easier to recognize than to practise, particularly when the picture being presented in a report is critical, unfavourable or unsatisfactory. It is very tempting for a line manager to take the easy way out and produce a "good" or "satisfactory" report for a member of staff whose performance is anything but satisfactory. Being objective and impartial can result in the reporting officer facing a difficult discussion with the staff member. If, however, reports are *not* objective, accurate, impartial and unbiased, the organization cannot rely on them for the purposes set out above.

Staff reporting procedures should be designed in such a way that the risk of subjectivity, partiality or bias is minimized. This can be done in a number of ways but a method commonly used is to require more than one line manager to take part in the reporting process. This involves "two (or three) tier" reporting. The first tier — the staff member's immediate supervisor or line manager — is the reporting officer and the one who completes the report. The second tier — the reporting officer's immediate line manager — will then examine the completed report; question, challenge and discuss with the reporting officer any assessments or comments with which he disagrees and, once any necessary changes have been made, countersign the report. In organizations where a third tier is also used it will be the counter-signing officer's immediate line manager who further examines the report.

In theory, such a system should ensure a far higher level of objectivity, accuracy and impartiality. This can only be achieved in practice, however, if *all* line managers involved in the reporting process adopt the highest standards at all stages of the reporting process. It is also important to recognize that the system can work satisfactorily *only* if line managers know their staff very well; regrettably this is not always the case.

It will be apparent that the reporting process is retrospective, for a report refers to the performance of the job over the past year. It will also have been clear that the officer being reported on has a passive role in the process; *all* the responsibility rests with line managers — the reporting and counter-signing officers.

Appraisal reviews

Appraisal reviews (sometimes also referred to as job appraisal reviews or performance appraisals) are normally an annual event and are significantly different to staff reports in two ways. First, although they do have regard to performance of the job and what has been achieved in the past year, they also focus heavily on the year ahead. Secondly, the member of staff whose performance is being appraised plays a major part in the process.

The purpose of the appraisal review is to assist individual members of staff to carry out their job to the best of their ability and to ensure that their capabilities are recognized and their potential developed to the full.

The appraisal interview provides an opportunity for the staff member to discuss their job with their line manager. The discussion will include what the job entails, how it has been performed, what areas of the work are found to be difficult, what problems are encountered day to day. It should also provide encouragement for the member of staff to plan how to better their performance, how to capitalize on strengths and minimize any weaknesses, to put forward and develop ideas for improvement of individual performance and for that of their section or department. It is also an opportunity to discuss ways in which experience can be widened.

What is important — and this further emphasizes one of the key differences between reporting and appraisal — is that it is a *two-way* process. There must be an effective exchange and interchange of opinions and ideas. From appraisal interviews, "senior" officers need to get a clear picture of how "junior" officers see themselves, in relation both to their current job and its future performance. The "junior" officers want to know how their contribution to the organization is seen and evaluated.

The objectives of appraisal may be stated as follows:

- to enable individual members of staff to discuss performance in the job, for the year under review, with their line manager;

- together with the line manager, explore and agree ways of improving that performance in the coming year;

- to provide an occasion for the member of staff to take part in decisions which affect him/her, by -
  - making suggestions about aspects of the job which experience suggests might benefit from a change in structure or organization,
  - putting forward ideas for his/her job experience and future career.

This section of the unit began by pointing out that the terms "reporting" and "appraisal" are often used (wrongly) interchangeably. However, not only is it important to be aware of the difference, it is also very important not to confuse the processes. Some organizations attempt to intermix the two, for example by producing an annual staff report, using that as a vehicle for an interview with the staff member, and then calling the combined action "an appraisal".

Because they have different aims and objectives, even though they are clearly related, it is desirable to keep the two systems separate and distinct, although operating in parallel.

This section on reporting and appraisal would not be complete without reference to the need, within an organization, for uniformity of standards. This can be achieved in several ways. For example the requirement of some reporting systems to use two or more "tiers" assists middle and senior line managers to maintain common standards of reporting. A major contribution to uniform standards can be made by providing reporting officers, and those responsible for appraisal reviews, with high quality training. This should be supplemented by written guidance on reporting and appraisal, which is invaluable as a permanent source of reference and which can be used repeatedly.

E. Career development

Section C of this unit offeded some definitions of and made some distinctions between "training, education and development", and then went on to deal in some depth with training; Section D examined staff reporting and appraisal. The unit has, therefore, already covered much of what is to be said about career development; for training, reporting and appraisal are three of its key features.

Career development has benefits for, and is important to, both the individual and the organization. It involves the management of an individual's career in order to ensure development and career satisfaction. Concurrently, and equally importantly, career development helps to meet the personnel needs of the organization. For example, ensuring that someone has a planned rotation of jobs over a number of years not only helps to develop and motivate the individual but also enhances the organization's flexibility.

Specifically, career development aims to:

- help staff to identify the competences which they need for current and future jobs;

- help align and integrate personal objectives with organizational objectives;

- help develop new career paths which point outwards for the individual — not necessarily only "upwards";

- revitalize those employees who may be stagnating in their careers or present job;

- provide opportunities to employees to develop themselves and their careers to the mutual advantage of the individual and the organization.

A positive career development policy will also enable the organization to identify those who show potential for promotion, and provide opportunities for training to be given and experience gained in preparation for the higher grade. In this way, the organization can help to ensure succession and have people ready to step into supervisory, middle or senior management posts as they become vacant.

Career development therefore needs to involve the following processes:

- systematically monitoring and assessing the potential of staff (largely through reporting and appraisal procedures);

- producing career plans for individuals, particularly those who display potential, to ensure that they have the mix of experience and training which will equip them for whatever level of responsibility they have the ability to reach;

- providing career advice and guidance for individuals on -

  - how to acquire the necessary knowledge and skills to do a new or different job,

  - how to deal with work problems;

- giving coaching in specific skills, and help in tackling projects.

To introduce and operate an effective career development policy requires a great deal of effort and commitment by each member of the management team, at all levels of the organization. This represents a huge investment of resources but the returns for the organization will more than repay that investment.

UNIT 2: Monitoring performance

A. Statistics

Statistics are an essential feature of almost all management activities and form the basis of many management decisions. Social security institutions devote considerable time and effort to the collection of statistics, which are then used in a multitude of ways. Those which are used internally relate to a wide variety of activities including budgeting, financial monitoring and forecasting, staffing needs, assessment of performance, accuracy levels, clearance times, etc. All social security institutions are accountable, directly or indirectly, to government and are usually required to produce statistics relating to income and expenditure, and to publish accounts. This cannot be done without the extensive collection of statistical information.

As with all other aspects of management, there is a need for great care when decisions are taken on the range and type of statistics which are to be collected and maintained. It is all too easy to introduce a new set of statistics on a particular operation, organizational function, or aspect of the work, without giving adequate thought to the impact on the staff who will be involved in collecting and maintaining the data. Before a new set of statistics is introduced there must always be a specific need, which can only be met by them and they must always serve a particular purpose. If statistics are not meaningful, the time spent on collection and recording will be time wasted.

It is not sufficient simply to instruct staff to maintain a given set of statistics; they must understand *why* they are being asked to keep them and *how* those statistics will be used. Statistics are often carelessly or inaccurately recorded and poorly maintained — in which case, of course, they are unreliable. This is very often due to the fact that the training of staff in the collection, maintenance and use of statistics is neglected.

Another factor which impacts on the accuracy and quality of statistical information is the format of documents on which they are recorded. If statistical forms are complex, poorly designed, difficult to understand and complete, then errors will be frequent. If, however, they are well set out, easy to understand and use, then the likelihood of incorrect completion will be reduced and the reliability of the statistical information recorded thereon increased.

Fig. 26:
"... if you don't come up with some impressive statistics soon ... you'll be adding to this months unemployment figures ...!"

Whenever new statistical returns are introduced by the organization, staff need to understand *why* they are being asked to "do extra work", for this is often what the maintenance of statistics is seen to be. Correct and postive attitudes will not be adopted to the new statistics unless such explanations are provided. Little value can be placed on statistics if a manager cannot be certain that they are accurate and reliable.

B. Targets and objectives

In many of the day-to-day activities of all social security institutions there is a need to identify specific objectives which must be met and to set particular targets in order to help achieve those objectives.

The "objectives" are the specific aims of an organization and should be set out in the form of performance targets for each particular function. A "target" is a quantified aim or result which has to be achieved, usually within a specific period of time.

In well-established social security institutions, targets and objectives are widely used, across a range of functions, throughout the organization. This includes operations which directly affect contributors and beneficiaries (e.g. collection of contributions and payment of benefits) and those which primarily affect the administrative functions of the institution (e.g. budgetary requirements and controls, operational costs, staffing levels, work outputs, etc.).

Objectives need to be as precise as possible, must be measurable and should also be related to time. For example, it is not sufficient for a manager to decide that "some improvement is needed in the processing time for benefit claims". He must set the aim more precisely, for example, to clear 75% of all claims within 10 days of receipt, and the remaining 25% within 14 days. He may also determine that this overall objective should be achieved by a particular point in time, for example, six months hence. On the way to achieving that objective, individual targets would need to be set — perhaps at monthly intervals — of a 50% level by the end of the first month, 65% at the end of month two, etc. It is then necessary for a week by week comparison to be made, of *actual* clearance times against the target times, in order to measure performance against objective. Failure to meet a target should raise questions about why it was not met, prompt any corrective action which may be required and, perhaps, result in a review of how appropriate or realistic is the target itself.

The use of targets and objectives thus enables individual managers to approach their work and discharge their responsibilities in a measured and controlled way rather than simply "leaving events to take care of themselves". It also ensures that, at all levels of the organization, managers are able to measure the performance of their sections or departments against previously determined requirements, identify shortcomings and take corrective action where possible. At the individual level, it often results in more specific requirements for work output and quality.

C. Performance indicators

Performance indicators — PIs — are a useful tool which can assist managers to take more effective action in the planning and decision-making process, and operational improvements. They can help to provide a clearer picture of the current situation and general trends but PIs need to be well chosen, generally accepted, sufficiently simple and meaningful.

A number of methodological questions need to be asked.

- Who are the users, what do they want/need to learn through the use of PIs?

- Is it better to begin with PIs that can be based on information which is already available, even if the first series thus obtained is incomplete as a result of gaps in the existing statistics, or

- is it preferable to decide first on a set of PIs that corresponds best to the requirements of the various users, regardless of the immediate availability of data? (Many would consider that the first approach should be followed and that, even if there are information gaps, it should still be possible to establish an initial set of PIs).

As to the use of the PI itself, it is also necessary to distinguish between PIs and statistics in general. The normal distinction is that, for a statistic to become a PI, two things are required:

- it must mean something (i.e. it must reflect a variable which is useful to note or measure) and

- it must be linked with other PIs so as to represent the relations between variables.

How many PIs are desirable?

Normally, it is better to have a smaller — and therefore more manageable — range. This provides managers with a more simple, overall view which is, however, still large enough to present a picture of what is happening and the implications thereof. It is important to strike a good balance between having too few and too many PIs.

One approach is to produce a hierarchy of PIs. First come a small set of fundamental indicators, representing those operational aspects which it is *essential* to highlight. Then comes a larger group which it is considered *necessary or desirable* to highlight.

Senior managers may therefore receive *only* those relating to key operational areas, whilst managers at middle or junior levels of the organization may require a broader range of PIs on more detailed aspects of the operations.

One danger, in selecting aspects of the operations for PIs, is to give priority to those operational features which are most easily measured. Less quantifiable features may be more important but harder to measure and it is sometimes tempting to exclude these from the range of PIs; that temptation should, however, be avoided. It should also be noted that too great a preoccupation with measurement can detract from the broader picture and occasionally even distort it.

Nevertheless, PIs are useful for two main reasons. They can enable comparisons to be made, from one "performer" to another; "performer" being an office, a department, a section or an individual. They rarely provide answers but they do raise useful and meaningful questions on operational features which then need to be looked at closely, particularly where the target and the PI are at variance.

EPILOGUE

The manual began by asking what should be expected of a social security administration. In working through the seven modules, it will have become clear that the answer to the question is that "a great deal is expected ...".

Given the diversity of and differences between social security schemes, it has clearly only been possible to adopt a very broad approach to the administration of social security. Hopefully, however, the manual has drawn attention to most of the main administrative features, has identified some of the potential problem areas, has prompted ideas for improved administrative techniques and has encouraged innovative approaches to some of the administrative challenges facing social security institutions.

Throughout the manual, it has been acknowledged that lack of space prevented more detailed examination of the topics, but this was inevitable, given the range and volume of the administrative functions referred to. Each could fully justify a manual in its own right.

With those observations in mind, it is perhaps useful to close by repeating the response given at the beginning of the manual to the question "What should be expected of a social security administration?" ... any administration exists for one purpose only — **to provide an effective and efficient service for its clients**.

FURTHER READING

International Labour Office
Social security: a workers' education guide
Geneva, ILO, 1992, 113 p. ISBN 92-2-108004-8

Cichon M, Samuel L; ILO Central and Eastern European Team,
Budapest;
Cyprus. Ministry of Labour and Social Insurance;
Making social protection work: the challenge of tripartism in social governance for countries in transition
Budapest, ILO-CEET, 1994, 265 p. (Cyprus Round table on the Design and Governance of Social Protection Systems, Larnaca, 23-25 March 1994) ISBN 92-2-109740-4

International Social Security Association
Accountability of the partners in social security
Geneva, ISSA, 1995, 102 p. (Social Security Documentation: European Series, no. 24).
ISBN 92-843-1097-0

UK. Department of Social Security (London, DSS, 1997):
Research Report ...
  No. 63, **Exploring customer satisfaction**
    Elam G, Ritchie J; 90 p. ISBN 0-11-762468-3
  No. 65, **Customer contact with the Benefits Agency**
    Stafford B, Kellard K, Horsley E; 240 p.
    ISBN 0-11-762533-7
  No. 68, **Claimants' perceptions of the claim process**
    Ritchie J, Chetwynd M; 100 p.
    ISBN 0-11-762541-8
  No. 69, **Delivering benefits to unemployed people**
    Kellard K, Stafford B; 115 p. ISBN 0-11-762553-1

D'Haene Y, Oudghiri M; International Social Security Association
Training and further training of managers and officials of social security institutions in a computerised work environment
Geneva, ISSA, 1993, 58 p. (24th ISSA General Assembly, Acapulco, 1992: Report XXI)

International Social Security Association
Social security and its users: from red tape to information access
Geneva, ISSA, 1993, 210 p. (Studies and Research, no. 33)
ISBN 92-843-1065-2 p. 23-45: R. Poirrier, Public information provided by social security institutions: current practice.

Ross JL et al. (United States General Accounting Office)
Social security administration: effective leadership needed to meet daunting challenges
Washington DC, GAO, 1996, 28 p. (HEHS 96-196)

International Social Security Association; 7th International Conference on Data Processing in the Field of Social Security, The Hague, 1994
Communication as a prerequisite for the integration of technological resources
Geneva, ISSA, 1995, 208 p. (Social Security Documentation)
ISBN 92-843-1087-3

International Social Security Association
25th ISSA General Assembly (Nusa Dua, 1995)
International Social Security Review 49(2), 1996, 5-126
[The report on the 26th General Assembly, Marrakech, 1998, is scheduled to appear in *International Social Security Review* 52(2), 1999]. See also the following reports:
> **No. III**, The importance of statistics in social security: A comparative evaluation of the efficiency of benefits (1996, 38 p.)
> **No. VI**, Complaints procedures in the field of social security (1996, 44 p.)
> **No. XX**, Communication and the quality of service provided (1996, 54 p.)
> **No. XXI**, Administrative decentralization and deconcentration (1996, 43 p.)

Bloch FS
Assessing disability: a six-nation study of processing disability pension claims and appeals.
International Social Security Review 47(1), 1994, 15-35

International Social Security Association; 8th International Conference on Data Processing in Social Security, Berlin, 22-24 October 1996
Innovations in information technology: a decisive factor in the further development of social security systems
Geneva, ISSA, 1996, 250 p. ISBN 92-843-1118-7

International Social Security Association;
Conferencia Interamericana de Seguridad Social
ISSA and CISS joint conference on re-engineering of social security organizations = Conferencia conjunta de la AISS y la CISS sobre la reingeniería des las instituciones de seguridad social = Conférence conjointe AISS et CISS sur la reconfiguration des institutions de sécurité sociale = Gemeinsame IVSS/CISS-Konferenz über die Reorganisation der Träger der sozialen Sicherheit
Geneva, ISSA, 1997, 1 vol. (Washington, 3-6 June 1997)

International Social Security Association
Third meeting for directors of social security organizations in the Pacific
Geneva, ISSA, 1997, 1 binder (Pacific/RM/97)
Includes the papers "Public relations and social security", "Responsibilities of bodies governing social security schemes", and national reports on "Public relations as a tool for client satisfaction"

Lasseni Duboze S (ed.);
12th African Regional Conference, Libreville, Gabon, 10-13 Dec. 1996
Geneva, ISSA, 1996, 1 binder
Contains the papers "Improving the administrative systems of social security institutions" (Gruat JV; Lasseni Duboze S), "Informing the public in order to make social security better known" (Bimpong KO; Zunon Kipre V), "The management of social security by the social partners in a framework of sound governance" (Katembe A; Khalfaoui R).

Miller G, Holstein JA
Dispute domains and welfare claims: conflict and law in public bureaucracies
London, JAI Press Ltd, 1996, 280 p. (Contemporary Ethnographic Studies, no. 8)
ISBN 0-7623-0084-1

Verstraeten J
Developments of management information systems: toward new information processing technology
Social Security Documentation: Caribbean Series (7), 1996, 7-54

Social Security Programs Throughout the World
Social Security Administration, Office of Research and Statistics.
(SSA Publication No.13-11805, July 1997)
ISBN 0-16-048224-0

www.ingramcontent.com/pod-product-compliance
Lightning Source LLC
Chambersburg PA
CBHW080841270326
41927CB00013B/3060